ISBN: 978-0-6481884-1-4

Copyright© 2018 MSI Australia
All rights reserved.

Published by Planet Press International Ltd.,
under licence from MSI Ltd, Australia
Company Registration No: 121 353 106
NSW, Australia

See our website: www.booksforreadingonline.com

Or contact by email: sales@booksforreadingonline.com or: admin@booksforreadingonline.com

Front & Back Covers and Copyright owned by MSI, Australia

MSI acknowledges the author of the images used in this book.

Photography by Christine Thompson-Wells ©

BOOKS
FOR READING
ONLINE

This book forms part of the CPD Accredited Course for Fast Track Commercial Floristry Course

FULL
POTENTIAL
TRAINING

CPD
CERTIFIED
The CPD Certification
Service

Welcome to this book of
How to Create
Easy Wedding Bouquets

In the following pages you will be given step-by-step direction on how to create a number of different wedding bouquets. There are over 180 diagrams and over 100 photographs to help you learn the techniques spoken about within the pages of the book.

You will gain information about how to construct bouquets that are affordable to make. You will also learn more about colour, texture, shape, form and placement.

Wedding flowers have been used for thousands of years. Ancient Rome and Greece were known for their floral festivals. During those times, the use of red roses combined with purple violets symbolised the cycle of life and death. During the Middle-Ages herbs such as dill were combined with some hedgerow flowers, these were made into informal bouquets. Dill and garlic were also added to the festivity garlands supposedly to arouse the couple to become ready to consummate their marriage later that night.

During the 1930s wedding bouquets were large but light in appearance with light, feathery flowers such as gypsophila (baby's breath) and asparagus fern being used. During the 1940s, due to the Second World War, many bouquets were made of gladioli which the bride would carry as an arm spray. These bouquets were held securely with large silk or satin bows.

Wedding bouquets appear to reflect the economy of the time in which the wedding takes place. In the early 1980s, Princess Diana's wedding bouquet was large and made using the traditional Constance Spry methods, whereas, Catherine Middleton's wedding bouquet of 2011 was small and compact, this possibly reflecting the global recession of 2008.

Every wedding that takes place around the world does so because of human emotions and the feelings that two people have towards each other. A wedding is a rite of passage and to the two people involved, it is a very important experience. This is why, when a person is asked to make a wedding bouquet, it is both a compliment and a belief of trust that the florist has the experience and knowledge to carry out the wishes of the bride.

If you loved our last book: **How To Create Easy Flower Arranging**, you will love How **To Create Easy Wedding Bouquets**.

The book contains step-by-step instruction in HOW TO make a range of different Bouquets. It contains over 108 colourful photographs, and over 180 figurative drawings for you to follow.

It's easy to learn the *industry secrets* with this **NEW** approach to an age old art form.

About The Author

*C*hristine Thompson-Wells trained as a florist in London.

She has owned and run many successful florist shop businesses and taught many students in her own floristry school and taught floral design, art, commercial floristry, visual merchandising and many other subjects at the Canberra Institute of Technology; she is also a qualified educator.

Christine, because of the need for florists to enter the workforce, initiated the commercial floristry course in1984 at Canberra Institute of Technology where the course is still running at Bruce Campus, Bruce, Canberra in the Australian Capital, Australia.

She says, 'the course took four long years to bring to fruition but, thankfully, it's still running in 2018.'

After selling one of her businesses, Christine was appointed as the florist for the Prime Minister and Mrs Fraser at the Prime Minister's Lodge, Canberra, Australia. During that time she created the floral arrangements for one of the Queen's visits to Australia; she has been a writer for Flora International where her work was published to a worldwide audience.

Feeling the need to know more, after selling one of the businesses, Christine went to university to study Education and Psychology. She says, 'the reason I went to university was that I wanted to know why people bought flowers?' This question has led her on to do a great deal of writing and has had many books and articles published on the study of human behaviour. She writes within a large genre which includes: children's books, books on mind health and wellbeing, poetry and a range of other subjects.

Content   Page

To Begin

Most wedding bouquets for the bride are made by another person. This person may be the florist in the home town, friend, future mother-in-law or the lady who grows roses and lives at the end of the bride's street!

The most important point to remember: flowers are carried by the bride as an ancient tradition. Many brides carry only one wedding bouquet in their life, therefore the emphasis placed on the bouquet is paramount to the bride.

The cost of the wedding bouquet is a consideration for most brides. If you are creating a wedding bouquet, you will need to understand, the bride will have her preferences to the flowers she wants but availability and expense need to be spoken about in the very early stages of taking a wedding order. Be kind and understand a bride with empathy and your job will become easier.

Simple tips

1. Keep the ideas simple.

2. Do not offer flowers that are out of season. Always consider the availability of the flowers being spoken about by the bride.

3. Always take a second choice. Do not take one choice only.

4. Consider the colours the bride is speaking about.

5. Remember, white is a tint and black is a shade – so many professional florists have this wrong. Soft pink, pale lemon, soft blue, pale lavender are tints of colours because the colours have white combined. Whereas, deep red, deep blue, deep purple are shades because the colours have black combined.

6 Ask the bride for swatches of material; you will need these to match colours of the flowers and to see if the colours of the flowers available match the chosen fabric

7 Order your flowers early from the grower. If possible, let your grower or supplier know many weeks in advance the type, colour and quantity of flowers you will need.

8 Keep the bride informed of your progress. Availability and changes to wedding flowers should be told to the bride as soon as possible. Or better still, if you are in doubt about possible flowers or colours, inform the bride: 'I will do my best.'

9 Make sure your sundry items ribbons etc are prepared and ready for use before you start making the bouquet work.

Before Making Your Bouquets – Please Read Every Instruction Carefully.

Read It Once, Twice Or Three Times If You Need To... The Content Needs To Be Understood.

The Tools You Will Need

1.

2.

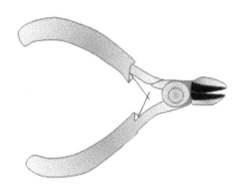

Secateurs

(1) Use secateurs or flower cutters to cut your flowers. Cutting with scissors will squash the tiny stem cells as they cut through the stem.

3.

Wire Cutters

(2) Good wire cutters are a valuable asset. Keep them on your bench and close to your work as you prepare your flowers and create your wedding bouquet.

4.

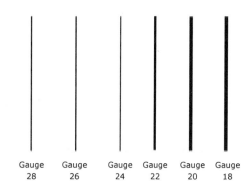

| Gauge 28 | Gauge 26 | Gauge 24 | Gauge 22 | Gauge 20 | Gauge 18 |

Sharp Scissors

(3) Use sharp scissors for cutting ribbons and all bridal ribbons. Blunt scissors will fray your ribbon and cutting with blunt scissors makes hard work.

Keep ribbon scissors away from any other cutting tools and use only these scissors for cutting ribbon. Do not cut flowers or wires with ribbon cutting scissors.

Wire Gauges of Two Lengths:

9 inch (23cm) and 18 inch (46cm)

(4) Many people underestimate the value of florist wire. I've used it for making wire sculptures, creating thousands of wedding bouquets, fixing children's toys, searching for the end of a piece of string that is down a tube and other numerous jobs.

More seriously, knowing how to use florist wire properly in constructing wedding bouquets will pay dividends in saving you time, stress and expense.

Florist wires come mainly in two lengths, that of: 18" (46cm) or 9" (23cm) approximately. If you buy 18" length wire you can readily cut it to your desired length. Buying 9" (23cm) length wire is a little more restrictive but does allow for easy working with if there is a great deal of wiring to do with many wedding bouquets to make.

As outlined in diagram (4) above, the wires come in different gauges.

Using Florist Wire

28 gauge wire is suitable for wiring of fine leaves, pinning up the sepals of roses and other fine work. As you go through the book, I will discuss many of these aspects within wiring work.

26 gauge wire is suitable for wiring fine flowers for corsages, headdress design and other fine work.

24 gauge wire is suitable for wiring up larger flowers such as smaller carnations and roses, daisies and in some double-leg wiring such as wiring small gardenias.

22 gauge wire as suggested by the gauge number, the wires are now getting into heavier wires which are suitable for larger flowers or pieces of foliage or in places where firm control of the placement is needed. This wire is ideal for wiring larger, heavier roses, strong sim carnations, cymbidium orchids and in some instances double-leg wiring.

20 gauge wire as the gauge indicates, this wire is strong and not easy on the hands when a lot of wiring is required. This is why I often use double-leg wiring

when making some wedding bouquets. I will talk about double-leg wiring as you go through the book. The 20 gauge wire is a good supporting wire when large (all wired) bouquets are made. Again, I will talk about this aspect of wedding bouquet making as you go through the book.

18 gauge wire is a strong wire that is used when shapes in wedding work are made. Florist wire is often used to create different shapes such as a heart-shape bouquet design. The flowers of the bouquet sit in the middle of the heart shape; it's a very beautiful design but a lot of work; not mentioned in this book.

The Principles Of Wiring

The following principle is ideal for some light-weight flowers used in wedding work, corsage and headdress design and where the flowers are playing a supporting role in the design.

Single-leg hooked method

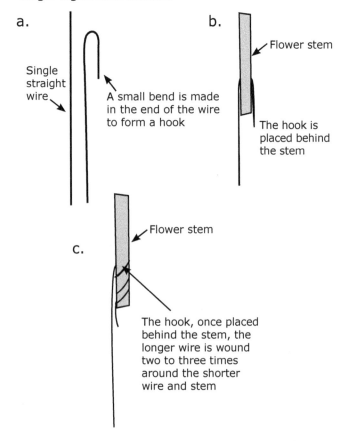

a.

Single straight wire

A small bend is made in the end of the wire to form a hook

b.

Flower stem

The hook is placed behind the stem

c.

Flower stem

The hook, once placed behind the stem, the longer wire is wound two to three times around the shorter wire and stem

With diagrams (a), (b) and (c) on page 3.

a) Take a single wire
b) Bend a 'U' shape in one end of the wire, this forms a hook
c) Place the stem you want to secure the wire to in front of the 'U' shape and bring the longer leg of wire around the stem and shorter piece of wire. You now have a flower stem attached to a piece of florist wire.

As you learn to wire leaves and flowers, do not allow your wires to cross over as shown in diagram (d) below.

In diagram (d), it can be seen in how the wire is crossed over previously wound wires. This habit not only looks unsightly, it adds to the look of your work being unprofessional.

d.

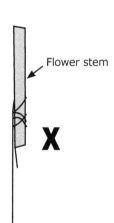

← Flower stem

X

Double-leg, hairpin wiring is ideal for pinning flowers or foliage into a solid base as in wreath work or where the wire can act as a supporting wire in the floral design.

For example, if you are pinning down heavy foliage in the construction of a wreath, you will need a 20 or 18 gauge wire; if you are going to use this wire shape in delicate headdress construction to secure a piece of baby's breath (gypsophila) you will possibly need to use 28 or 26 gauge wire.

To give you more of an example: A 9 inch (23cm) wire can be cut in two making each wire 4 ½ inch (12.5cm) in length. This wire is then bent to form the hairpin shape. You will need to judge the thickness of the wire and its purpose.

Double-leg hairpin wiring use continued

Again, the wire is bent in two, this time, a single wire is wound around a stem giving extra support to it's placement in your design. Both legs will have a similar length.

b.

Single wire

In diagram (b) above, this wiring technique has its advantages when extra support is needed to hold flowers or foliage in place.

Double-leg hairpin wiring

a.

Single wire

The wire is bent in two and is ideal for holding flowers or foliage securely when placed into your design

A simple and fast technique

a. Double-leg vertical wire method

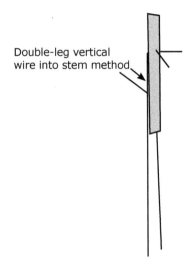

Double-leg vertical wire into stem method.

The Double-leg vertical wire stem method is a quick method of wiring and is ideal for wiring Gardenias.

Gardenia flowers have fleshy stems and can be simply taken from the calyx of the flower – they snap off with a little pressure when the stem is between your finger and thumb. In diagram (a) above, two vertical wires are inserted either side of the gardenia. The shorter wires are seen coming out in a horizontal direction.

In diagram (b) below, the shorter wires are brought down into the vertical position, no twisting of wires is necessary.

Double-leg vertical wire method

Once the wires are in place, then, parafilm stem tape both the stem and two wires together to form one stem.

For corsages, instead of inserting two wires as shown above, a single wire can be inserted into the calyx of the flower, both the stem of the rose and wire are parafilmed stem taped together forming one stem. Please see below

Single-leg wire for calyx wiring

Single-leg for calyx wiring

a.

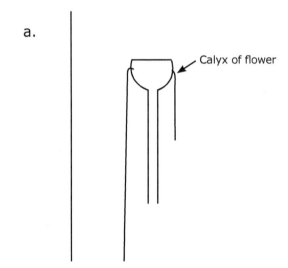

Calyx of flower

The calyx is the outside green structure that includes the sepals. This structure protects the ovaries and allows for fertilisation ensuring the flowers future and continued existence.

This method of wiring is ideal for headdress and corsage design. In diagram (a) above I'm using a rose shape calyx as an example. Once you have chosen the flower and the appropriate wire, push the wire through the calyx until it penetrates and comes through the opposite side. Keep this wire short. Turn the wire down as seen in the above diagram.

This type of wiring is suitable for some rose and carnation placements or other flowers that have a protruding calyx.

Single-leg wiring for calyx wiring

b.

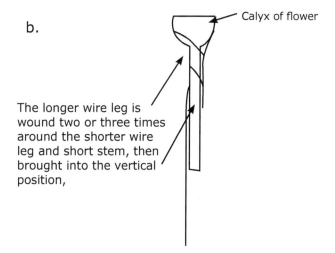

Calyx of flower

The longer wire leg is wound two or three times around the shorter wire leg and short stem, then brought into the vertical position,

The wiring techniques spoken of are used in bouquet, corsage making and wreath construction.

Diagram (b) shows thewires wound around the short wire and stem. Once this is done, parafilm stem tape the stem and wire giving the appearance of one stem.

To create and feel satisfied with the work you are constructing, you will need to work with all of the gauges of wires spoken of in the above – do practice runs before creating the piece of work you need to work on.

Single-leg hooked wire – leaf wiring

a.

Single-leg - hooked wire in leaf wiring

Seen in (a), opposite page, is a single leaf and a 26 gauge x 9 inch (23cm) wire in the vertical position.

In (b) below, the diagram shows the shorter end of the wire penetrating the backbone or vein of the leaf.

b.

The wire is inserted through the backbone or vein of the leaf. The shorter and penetrated leg of the wire measures about ¼ of the overall and remaining length of wire.

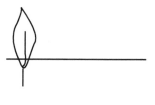

In (c), the shorter length of wire is bent downwards into the vertical position.

c.

The wire is inserted through the backbone or vein of the leaf. The short leg of wire measures about ¼ of the overall length of wire.

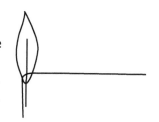

The shorter wire and small stem are now ready to be wound into place by the longer leg of wire, seen in red. This encases both the short stem and wire.

In diagram (d) below, the wire is in position and the stem and wire are ready to be parafilm stem taped together, this forming one leg.

d.

The wire is inserted through the backbone or vein of the leaf. The short leg of wire measures about ¼ of the overall length of wire.

The wired leg is now ready for placement into your design.

Single-leg, hooked wire method

Select the wire weight you are going to use; the wires need to be soft enough to penetrate in to and through the flower base.

(a)   A straight wire is seen
(b)   At the top of the wire, a small portion is parafilmed stem taped
(c)   Shows the hooked wire with a parafilm stem taped bend. This bend faces upwards once the wire penetrates the flower
(d)   The wire bend sits snugly in the centre of the flower
(e)   The stem end and wire are parafilmed stem taped together forming one secure wired flower
(f)   In diagram (f), more than one flower is mounted on a single wire; this method of construction allows one placement with multiple flowers...
      If the flower heads appear too heavy for the one wire, support it by placing a vertical wire parallel with the lowest floret.

d

The wire bend sits snugly in the centre of the flower

e

The wire and stem end are parafilmed taped together

Hooked wire method supports three small flower florets

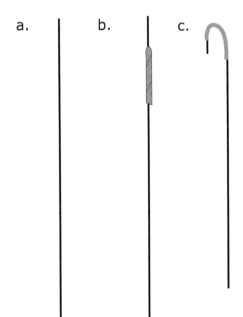

a.   b.   c.

Hyacinth florets can become too heavy for one wire leg. If this is the case, add a second supporting wire. The wire is simply placed at the base of the third lower flower, the two wires and short lower, hyacinth flower stem are secured by binding all three with parafilm stem tape.

g.

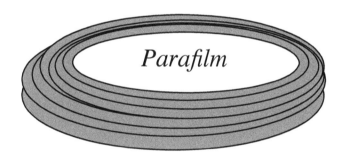

Diagram (g) shows the supporting wire prior to parafilm stem tape added.

Supporting wire is inserted into the base of the flower - both wires and short flower stem are the parafilmed

Parafilm

Parafilm stem tape is mainly sold in green. In some instances, brown and white can be bought.

There is a definite skill to using Parafilm stem tape. When first using it, remember to 'stretch the tape and pull,' wind, when stretched onto the flower stem and wire. **'Stretch, Pull, Wind'** Repeat these words in your head:

'Stretch, Pull, Wind.'

Parafilm stem tape

Parafilm stem tape is used by florists in many countries worldwide. Binding a stem with parafilm stem tape, which is a plastic-based tape, aids in keeping the stem end moist when placed into position in the wedding bouquet. Parafilm stem tape also allows the wired stem to stay secure and in place once it's in position in the bridal design.

Some Tools You May Prefer To Use

Bridal floral foam bouquet holder or Bridie

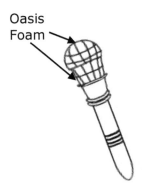

Oasis Foam

Green oasis is within the cone at the top of the holder. The complete holder is soaked in water prior to the construction of the bouquet.

Many florists still use the above holder; I will demonstrate how this is used later in the book.

When I first started my floristry training, some of the bouquets were constructed on a wired, ball of moss; the bridal bouquet holder has taken over from this old method.

For speed, I use just wire in the construction of my wedding work.

Other Tools

<u>Silver and Coloured</u> wire is handy to have close to your hands when you're in the middle of bouquet construction, especially if you want to add a bit of difference to your work.

<u>Head Pins</u> In the construction of corsages and buttonholes, you will need a variety of headpins. People wear so many different colours, it's nice to match the pin with the colour of the flowers or colour in the clothes the customer is wearing on the day of the occasion. The pin allows the flowers to be attached to the customer's clothes and is usually worn on the shoulder; having said that, there is a trend to corsages being worn on the customer's wrist. This was fashionable in the 1960s. This resurgence is now available and made by many florists. The corsage is made while being attached to a pre-made bracelet. The bracelets can be bought at many market wholesalers, or on line.

Another idea for corsage attachment is variety of different shaped diamante buckles. Many of the accessories can be bought through online websites under the heading of florist wholesale sundries.

<u>Clear Elastic Bouquet Tying Tape</u> Now available and is a binding tape in clear plastic. This clear tying tape is a tool no florist should be without; it saves time, frustration and stress.

<u>Glue guns</u> are a very usable tool in many flower arrangements these days – they are handy to have on hand when you are creating wrist corsages, some headdress designs, some shoulder corsages, Christmas and wreath arrangements.

If you need to or are thinking about buying a glue gun for your floristry work, I suggest you buy a gun with a fine nozzle. A fine nozzle helps when adding small flowers, foliage or sundry items to headdress, corsage or wedding work.

Creating the Focal Area Of Your Design

The Focal Area of all design work, from bouquet to arrangement making is often not understood.

All floral arrangements have focal areas. Whether you are creating a mass design for a church or cathedral festival, to simple wedding bouquets or bouquets of complex design – all have a focal area that needs to be known about and understood.

A focal area within any design is the area where the human eye can gently rest, take a pause and then resume its journey of enjoying the work created.

A focal area contains:

- Interest
- Fascination
- A place of emergence from where other flowers and foliage emerge
- Colour co-ordination and complexity
- Texture interest and weight and
- Eye appeal

In wedding bouquet construction, the focal area is where the junction of the handle is created. The focal area contains the fascination of the above points and more. This is why, it is important to mentally plan your design before making the design. A design without any thought will look like a design that is thrown together and the designer is hoping for a miracle to happen. Yes, sometimes miracles do happen, but if you are working for a client or customer you will need to understand that thinking your design through, before constructing the design, will save you money, time and headaches.

In the diagram below, the focal point is where all of the stems, including leaf stems, or material appear to radiate from.

By studying the diagram below, you will see that the anthurium lily flower shapes are turned slightly in size and progression meeting, with the larger flowers, towards the focal point.

A Self-stem bouquet showing the focal point

Focal point
of a wedding bouquet
is the centre of interest
within the design.

By understanding this technique, your designs will always have appeal and will appear well designed and visually balanced.

Creating Ribboned Handles For Wedding Bouquets –

The Looped Bow

Shown in diagram (a) below is the back of a fully made wedding bouquet.

a.

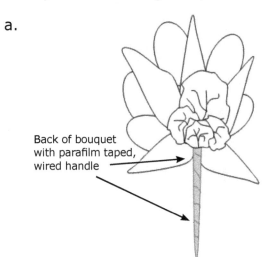

Back of bouquet with parafilm taped, wired handle

There are many ways to finish off wedding bouquet handles, as you become familiar with your own techniques, you will find a way that works for you.

In diagram (b), I've chosen the best ribbon to suite the bouquet colouring. Then I have estimated how much ribbon I will need to make a two-looped, ribbon bow; if you wish, you can leave the ribbon attached to the reel.

b.

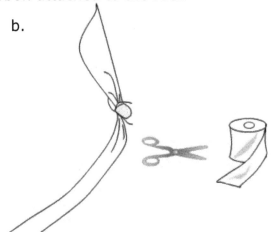

In diagram (c) below, the first of two loops has been added to the initial length. I keep securely between my thumb and index finger, the pinched ribbon end and loop.

c.

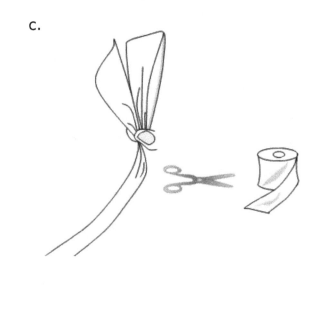

Diagram (d) shows the second loop in place. Keep the loops securely held between your thumb and index finger as you come to the end of making your bow.

d.

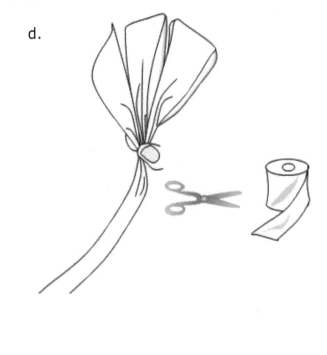

Diagram (e), the last unlooped part of the bow is twisted backwards to mirror the first pleated end and the excess ribbon is cut away. The bow is ready to be wired in the single-leg, hooked method.

e.

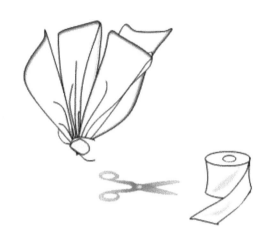

In diagram (g), the ribbon pleats are shown with the wire wound around the pleats which secure the bow into place.

g.

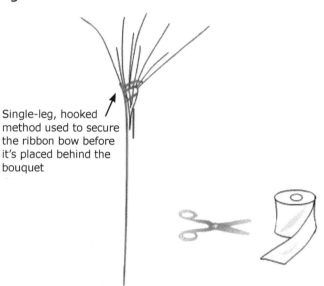

Single-leg, hooked method used to secure the ribbon bow before it's placed behind the bouquet

Diagram (f) below, shows the single-leg, hooked method of wiring with the hook of the wire ready to go behind the back of the bow.

f.

Single-leg, hooked method of wiring

In diagram (h), below, the parafilm stem tape is stretched, pulled and wound around the base of the made bow. It is wound tightly, 'stretching and pulling' and goes about ¾ of the way down the stem of the wire.

h.

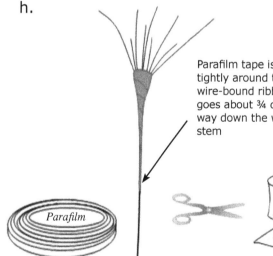

Parafilm tape is wound tightly around the wire-bound ribbon and goes about ¾ of the way down the wire stem

Parafilm

Diagram (i), below shows the bow, now parafilm stem taped, ready to be attached to the back of the wedding bouquet.

i.

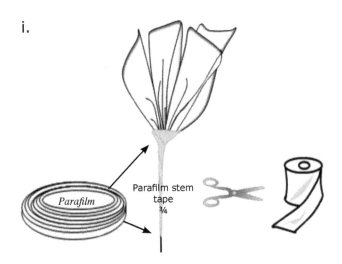

Parafilm

Parafilm stem tape ¾

Before attaching the first bow is attached to the bouquet handle, make sure you have the 5 or 6 completely ready.

In diagram (j), the first ribbon takes its place.

j.

The first wired bow is put into place; the remaining 5 or 6 are now attached to the parafilm stem taped wire bouquet handle

Please Note:

I attach my taped and wired bows by taping the wired leg of the ribbon bow to the existing wired handle of the bouquet. Diagram (k) below shows extra ribbon bows added to the back of the bouquet design.

k.

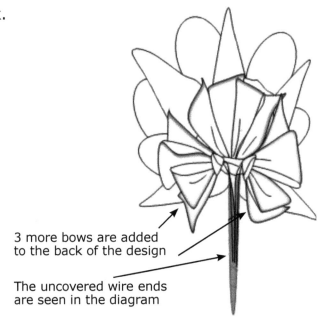

3 more bows are added to the back of the design

The uncovered wire ends are seen in the diagram

Diagram (l), shows the remaining ribbon bows in place.

l.

To Complete the Handle

In diagram (m), of the same ribbon the bows are made from, cut about ½ metre length; leave a small section of the ribbon showing, then pinch and create a small pleat, secure this pleat by inserting a pearl or diamante headpin which is pushed into the back of the bouquet.

m.

In diagram (o), the completed satin, ribboned handle. It's both pretty and comfortable for the bride or carrier of the bouquet to hold.

o.

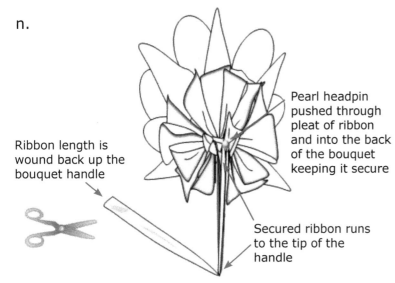

Pearl headpin secures the first ribbon end

In diagram (n) below, the length of ribbon is seen; with this end, you will wind it tightly around and up the bouquet hand. Then the remaining end is pinned into the back of the bouquet and the excess ribbon is cut off.

n.

Ribbon length is wound back up the bouquet handle

Pearl headpin pushed through pleat of ribbon and into the back of the bouquet keeping it secure

Secured ribbon runs to the tip of the handle

Pinned Bows

In diagram (a) below, a bunch of roses has been de-thorned and their stems are clean without any leaves; these roses are now acceptable to be tied into place to create a wedding bouquet. In some instances, you may wish to leave the leaves on the rose stems as I have done on page You can see further instructions for this design on page (22).

a.

Diagram (b) shows the rose stems tied tightly together in two places.

b.

Diagram (c) below shows parafilm stem tape pulled tightly around the stems after they are tied. Keep the parafilm stem tape pulled tightly under the heads of the roses.

c.

In diagram (d) a long length of ribbon is cut from the roll and pinned under the rose heads.

d.

Diagram (e) shows how the ribbon is pinned as it is taken up and down the length of the bouquet covering the rose stems. Use small headpins to put theses placements into place. You will use the stems as a base to secure the pins and the ribbon together.

e.

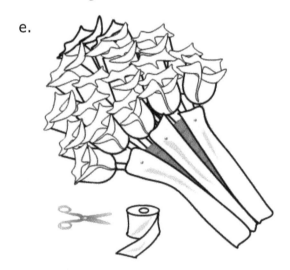

When adding the ribbon handle, keep the ribbon pulled as tightly as possible.

See the technique in diagram (f) below.

As I take the ribbon up and down, I carefully cover the bottom stem end ends.

When you have enough vertical strips covering your rose stems, you can start adding the loops under the roses as you go; these loops are secured with a finished headpin in pearl or diamante.

f.

Once you feel you have enough loops, which form the edging of the bouquet, you can start to wrap your ribbon horizontally as diagram (g) shows below

g.

To see the finished pinned bow, please see page (24).

In some instances, you may feel the bow needs a little something extra, at those times, and for finishing off, I tie a small bow in the back of the bouquet. To do this:

1. Cut a length of ribbon about 36 inches (91cm)
2. Lie the bouquet on the ribbon as in diagram (h) below.

h.

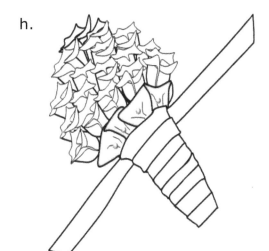

In diagram (i), the ribbon ends are
brought together to form a single, tight
knot.

i.

Tie the two ends into a pretty bow and
for the security of the ribbon, and as
seen in diagram (j), push a pearl or
decorative pin into the middle of the
bow.

j.

Bouquet Handles

Wedding bouquet handles should always be straight and easy to carry for the bride or the user. We often see handles that are curved like hooks or resemble a spiral shape. Have you ever watched the carrier of the bouquet? They fumble and fidget to keep the bouquet facing upwards and in the right direction. After all, a wedding bouquet must be a usable object and all objects of use should be easy to manage and comfortable to work with.

In diagram (a) below, the bouquet and handle are as one design. The flower and wire content of the bouquet should be of equal weight so that there is actual balance when the bouquet is carried.

a.

Part profile of a completed bouquet with a straight parafilmed stem taped handle in place

Handle of bouquet: straight and easy to hold

In (b) opposite, once the bouquet is completed and before the ribbon is attached to the handle, the weight of the bouquet can be tested by balancing the bouquet between the index finger and thumb; the bouquet, once the thumb is removed, should balance and stay in place on the index finger.

Balancing the bouquet

b.

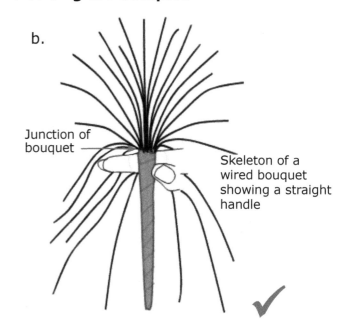

Junction of bouquet

Skeleton of a wired bouquet showing a straight handle

When A Bouquet Is Not Balanced

When a bouquet is not balanced it makes it difficult for the holder to carry or to feel comfortable holding. A balanced bouquet can be put out of balance by the following:

c. Profile and wire skeleton of a bouquet showing a wired and ribboned handle bent into a spiral shape allowing the bouquet to lose it's physical balance

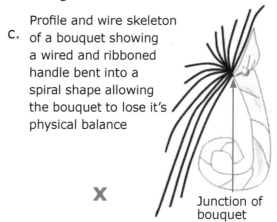

X

Junction of bouquet

18

In diagram (d) below, gravity takes over when designs aren't balanced. The bouquet will naturally want to fall forward because the physical equal balance has been removed by the bending of the handle.

The holder, usually the bride, will find the bouquet difficult to manage throughout the ceremony and the other important events such as photograph taking...

The only correct handle is the straight handle. A floral designer must think about the use and the user of the bouquet they are designing for. It's not any good saying, 'this is how we've always done this….' or 'that's my signature...' All floral designers need to live in the 'real world' when they are designing flower bouquets or any designs that are to be used or worn by a client or customer.

d.

Junction of bouquet

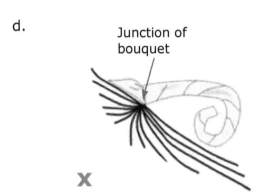

X

Diagram (e) below shows the bouquet with a less bent handle. Regardless of the bend in the handle, if it's not straight, the design will lose its physical balance and be difficult to use.

e.

A further example and profile of a bouquet wire skeleton and bent bouquet handled

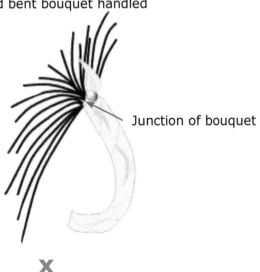

Junction of bouquet

X

Colour

For true colour to be seen it needs light. Colour has an emotional appeal which plays on our senses.

Colours are broken down as seen in the diagrams shown on this page.

1)

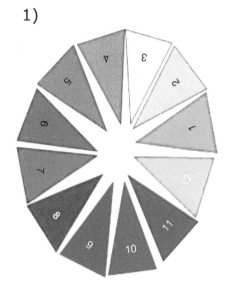

1	Green
2	Yellow-Green
3	Yellow
4	Yellow-Orange
5	Orange
6	Red-Orange
7	Red
8	Red-Violet
9	Violet
10	Blue-Violet
11	Blue
12	Blue-Green

2) **Primary Colours**

Red

Yellow

Blue

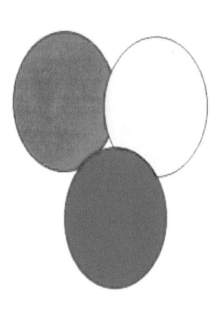

3) **Primary and Secondary Colours**

Red

Yellow

Blue

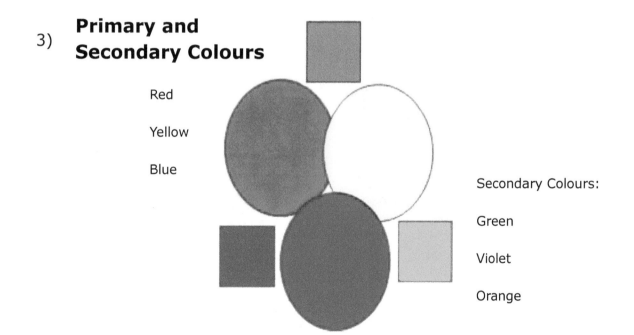

Secondary Colours:

Green

Violet

Orange

Texture

Like colour, texture does have expressive qualities. Surprisingly, there are both masculine and feminine qualities in texture. The masculine quality is seen in bark, knitting, hessian cloth; the petals of disbud chrysanthemum flowers, in many Australian native flowers and foliages and in other course or rugged surfaces.

Feminine texture is seen in the surface of chiffon, the surface of rose petals, on the petals of spring blossoms and other surfaces that are smooth to the touch or to the eye.

Understanding how texture works in flower arrangements and floral design is critical as texture can either add or take away, not only the visual balance, but also the appeal of your creation.

When talking about texture, we describe it as:

- Smooth
- Fine
- Medium
- Course and
- Rough

Large elements on the surface of the plant or flower will produce course texture and small elements will produce fine texture.

Your eyes will move slowly over course texture and rapidly over fine to smooth texture. If you like course or rough textures such as looking at bark, it creates in your mind a sense of slowness – stoppage points for the eyes to rest upon. When you look at a smooth texture, the smooth texture creates a visual sense of speed and allows your mind to be alert and clear.

If texture is an overpowering element, it can destroy what may have otherwise been a very good floral design. One of the obstacles to overcome in floral design is to understand the proportion of texture to colour. For example, when using white or light-coloured gerberas in a design a problem often arises. Gerberas are strong in texture but may be light in colour. I suggest the container should be strong in appearance but not necessarily in colour. A strong foliage, such as a broad-leafed, light in colour, Australian gum foliage can be used to balance and to give visual appeal to the floral arrangement if such dilemmas arise.

To give you some idea of the visual misleading messages texture can give to your visual senses, think of a single bird's feather. The texture of the feather is medium or course but appeals to our sense of touch. We know in our mind the softness and weight of the feather, therefore, the texture is misleading.

Getting to know and understand how texture plays such a vital role in all design work, including interior design, takes hours of thinking about and possibly years to learn. Having said this, the journey of recognising and working with texture brings magnificent rewards.

Easy and Simple Wedding Design
Hand-Tied, Self-Stem, Rose Posy

To begin any construction in wedding design, your materials must be well conditioned. Well conditioned applies not only to your flowers but also your foliage.

If you are using roses, as in the following design I am going to demonstrate how to make, make sure your roses and foliage feel strong in the stem, leaves and in the heads of the flowers. The roses I have bought are from the shop and were bought the day before they were used.

Flowers and foliage used in this design:

- 40 shop bought, small headed roses
- small leafed pittosporum foliage

One or two days before you use your flowers do the following:

Re-cut each stem end diagonally, as in diagram (a) below and separately and place immediately into deep water. Cutting the stem end in this way exposes more cell area and allows the flower more easily to take up water.

a.

The stem of a flower or leaf is cut horizontally. This exposes more cell area allowing easier water uptake.

1.

Leave the flowers and foliage in deep water, as in (1) the photograph above. Allow them to condition overnight, preferably in a cool place.

Make sure you are mentally ready to create the wedding bouquet. If your brain and mind isn't ready, your hands will not cooperate and you will end up with a disaster taking place.

Choose a beautiful rose for your main flower, please see the photograph (2) below. Make sure the flower is the best of the bunch...

2.

Once your flower is chosen, use tying tape to secure small pieces of foliage to the flower stem. You can make a foliage pad but I have not done this here. This technique is shown on page (32).

Profile of the first rose placement

3.

In photograph (3) above, you can see the rose and foliage stem are tied and secured together.

Now, grading the roses by size, slowly work more roses into the design.

When you feel you have enough flowers in place, tie the stems together.

b.

4.

In diagram (b) and photograph (4) above, the first tied section is in place.

In photograph (5) shows you how tightly put together the heads of the roses are placed.

5.

You will need to add more roses to make the full rose bouquet.

6.

In photograph (6) above, most of the roses have been added. Face your bouquet and look at squarely; even better, have a mirror handy to watch your hands and each flower as you put it into place.

Once the flower placements are all in place, securely and firmly tie the flower stems together to form one handle.

The self-stem bouquet handle

In photograph (7) below, the first and upper section of the bouquet is tied into place.

7.

Photograph (8) below shows the second tied section in place. This whole stem handle must be tight and firm to the touch, no movement is allowed in the handle of the bouquet.

8.

With the stems securely together, as seen in the above photograph (8), you can either bind the stems with parafilm stem tape or leave them as is shown in the above photograph.

For and against leaving exposed stems in wedding bouquet design work

i.   Exposed stems can give a natural look to the wedding bouquet
ii. There's always a possibility a thorn can be left on one of the rose stems, this may pierce the holders skin and cause bleeding
iii. Ribbon covered handles allows any unseen thorns to be covered
iv. Exposed rose stem ends can cause black, unmovable marking on light coloured fabric; this may ruin an expensive gown
v.   Ribbon covered ends are softer and nicer for the holder to carry and use
vi. Having the stems secured and covered by parafilm stem tape, then ribbon covered lessens the dehydration of the flowers, therefore, giving the flowers a longer life.

The profile of the almost finished bouquet shows how the ribbons add to the beauty of this simple design.

In photograph (9) below, you can see how neatly the ribbon handle sits with the profile of the rose buds.

9.

For more on Pinned Bows please see pages for 15 – 17.

10.

In photograph (10) opposite, the handle is bound with the same ribbon that is used to make the ribbon loops. When binding ribbon to bouquet handles, the ribbon must be pulled tightly as each bind is made. If you feel unsure about the security of the handle, discretely pin, with small headed pins in different places as you wrap the ribbon around the stem handle.

Hot Tip

Remove weather petals when cleaning and de-thorning your flowers prior to using them. (Weather petals are the torn and damaged petals on the outside of the rose that develop as the rose grows on the bush.)

Once the bouquet is made and before securing the ribbon, if it's excessively hot, you can sit the bouquet with water up to the neck of the roses to keep them fresh. Prior to adding the ribbon: remove the bouquet from the water, completely dry with a towel removing all moisture, then ribbon-up your bouquet.

Caution: if the roses are left too long in deep water, they may become soggy and water sodden.

Red Roses For Love

Hand-Tied, Self-Stem Bouquet Of White Carnations and Babies Breath

A combination of flowers can make a beautiful bouquet but too, can just two flower types make a lovely design. This bouquet of white carnations and babies' breath is yet another idea which shows that design is the key element in floristry work.

Flowers and foliage used in this design:

- 30 white carnations
- 2 bunches of babies' breath

Each of the carnations is wired through the bottom part of the calyx of the flower. Please see diagram (a). The wire is inserted in and through the lower part of the calyx.

a.

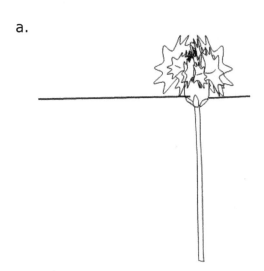

In diagram (b.) the wire end sections are turned downwards; the shorter section remains straight while the longer section is wound two or three times around the short section and carnation stem.

The red wound wire, shown in the diagram below, shows the wire is shorter than the carnation stem. This is done deliberately as the stem needs to be seen as a connected part of the bouquet and is part of the design.

b.

In photograph (1) below, and as outlined in the wiring techniques of (a) and (b), the carnation is seen with the wire in place.

1

Once wired, each carnation is parafilmed stem taped, prior to the bouquet being made. Once this id down, they are ready for use. As I work, I stand my flowers in a tall container. This method keeps the weight off the flower heads and stops bruising taking place.

In photograph (2) below, the flowers are wired and parafilm stem taped and are ready for use.

2.

To begin making the bouquet, I take the best flower in shape, form, texture and colour to be my first placement; this placement is in the centre of the bouquet. Please see diagram (c) below.

c.

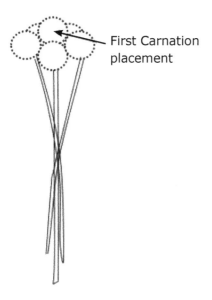

First Carnation placement

In (d) below, a number of carnations are in place.

d.

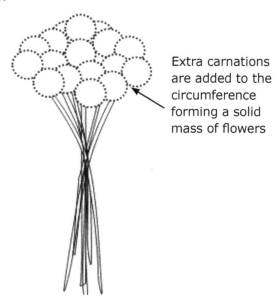

Extra carnations are added to the circumference forming a solid mass of flowers

As the mass of flowers accumulates, tie the mass firmly with plastic tying tape, bowl tape or a strong non-giving tying tape. Please see photograph (3) below. I've used clear plastic bouquet tying tape. This product is available on line at florist wholesalers.

3.

Continue to add your carnations keeping them tight without any spaces showing.

e.

More carnations
are added completing
the size, shape and
circumference of the
bouquet

In photograph (5) below, the mass as it
is seen front on.

5.

In diagram (e) above and photo (4)
below, the carnations mass has been
securely tied off. If, when the mass
doesn't feel secure, secure again with
extra tying tape.

4.

Once you are happy with your work it is
now time to add the babies' breath. Sort
through and look for strong lengths of
babies' breath; sort these out before
adding the flowers to your mass of
carnations. With sufficient pieces, you
are now ready to add the lengths. Please
see photograph (6) below

6.

As in the above photograph, the babies'
breath placements are also tied into
position.

To finish the bouquet handle you can follow the ideas on pages (15-17) or you can do the following:

f.

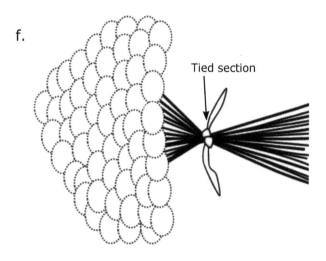

Tied section

In diagram (g) there are now two tied sections forming the handle of the bouquet.

As with many diagrams in this book, this is a diagrammatic illustration and the carnations you buy or use may vary in stem thickness, be uneven and gnarled, as many carnation stems are. Be aware of the stem sizes, their shape and the size of the handle they may produce.

g.

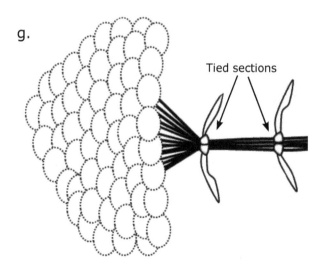

Tied sections

In diagram (h) stems of babies' breath have been added to the bouquet. Once all placements are in place, the stems are wound with parafilm stem tape then covered with ribbon leaving the stem ends free and showing.

h.

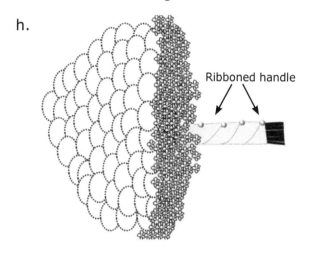

Ribboned handle

Please Note:

The choice of how we finish off bouquets is our choice; however, leaving bare stems ends exposed can lead to a dress or gown being damaged. The consequences can be far greater than taking the time to cover the stems and ends securely with ribbon.

Hot Tip

Design Master is a spray for locking in moisture and preserving flower life. Lightly sprayed on some wedding work can help to preserve your designs. Having said that: 'well conditioned flowers are the only ones that should be used in any wedding bouquets.'

Design Master is available online or through floristry sundry and wholesalers.

Soft And Beautiful

Hand-Tied, Self-Stem Bouquet Of Magnolia Leaves, White Dahlias And Yellow Rose Buds

To begin this design, you will need to find some pieces of durable foliage. I have 4 stems of green Magnolia leaves. You can use Camellia leaves or leaves that are of a similar density and substance. You are looking for a nice crown of foliage.

Flowers and foliage used in this design:

- magnolia leaves attached to the stem
- 6 white dahlias
- 5 stems of white spray chrysanthemums
- 30 small yellow roses
- 2 bunches of white babies' breath

Once you are happy with your foliage, you can start to assemble your flowers. Always, always make sure your flowers are well conditioned prior to making your design.

To begin, remove unwanted leaves from the lower stems of your base foliage, in this case, magnolia leaves. Leave a nice workable stem area. Tie the 4 or so stems together as in photograph (1).

1.

A diagram below showing the crown of foliage; when the crown is substantial, it makes placing the flowers easier.

a.

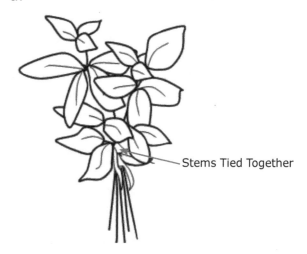

Stems Tied Together

In the beginning of this section on hand-tied bouquets, I spoke of the importance of the 'crown' of the foliage. In photograph (2) the crown is shown with a front and top view. This crown will form the outline and shape of your bouquet

2.

Each flower is prepared for its inclusion into the design prior to making the bouquet.

The dahlias have a wire inserted into the lower part of the calyx. The wire runs down and parallel with the stem – no twisting of the stem is necessary; I use just enough of a twist to keep the wire secure before I parafilm stem tape the wire to the stem. Please see photograph (3) below.

3.

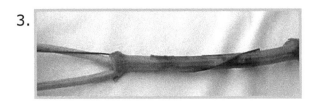

In photograph (4) below, you can see that some of the dahlia foliage has been left on the stem. By doing this, you are adding to the bulk of the bouquet.

4.

In diagram (a) below, outlined in red, it shows a 20 gauge by 9 inch (23 cm) length wire inserted into the base of the calyx. To finish the wire's attachment, I give a twist or two to keep the wire secure.

b.

Wire and parafilm stem tape all of your flowers prior to making your design. Once your flowers are wired and taped, they are ready for their placements within your bouquet.

The first flower placements are the white dahlias. Dahlias were once kept to garden flowers and very seldom seen in the cut flower markets but as the growers modify their growing and the production of flowers, many of these gems are becoming robust enough to use in the many areas of commercial floristry – dahlias are one such flower.

In photograph (5) below, the white dahlias are put into place; when you are happy with the placements, they can be tied into position.

5.

In diagram (c) below, the 6 white dahlias show up their perfect shape against the dark-green of the magnolia leaves.

c.

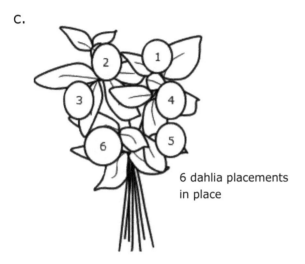

6 dahlia placements in place

In photograph (6) below, you can see the underside of the bouquet and its flower and foliage placements.

6.

The next placements are the stems of white chrysanthemums.
Chrysanthemums are usually sturdy in the stem and flower and don't need the supporting wires that many other flowers may need however, chrysanthemums, if not handled with care, will shatter; if this happens, the flower is unusable. Once shattering starts, the remaining petals will fall from the flower.

Photograph (7) below, shows the placements of the white dahlias and white chrysanthemums now securely placed within the design.

7.

Many progressions are made as you work with your design. No two flowers or pieces of foliage are ever the same so no two pieces of work that you do, regardless of how you try, will be identical. You can follow my guidelines but your work will have your distinctive signature.

In diagram (d) below, it shows the 5 stems of white spray chrysanthemums in place. These placements are kept to the perimeter of the design.

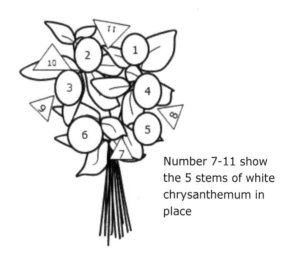

Number 7-11 show the 5 stems of white chrysanthemum in place

In diagram (e) below, the 30 small yellow Roses have been added. I have numbered them from 12-30 keeping the smaller buds and their shapes to the outside of the design.

e.

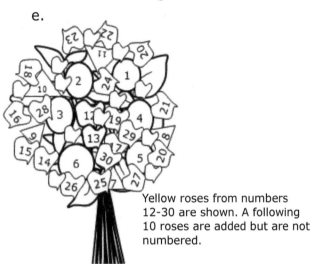

Yellow roses from numbers 12-30 are shown. A following 10 roses are added but are not numbered.

As your design takes shape, you will start to see the full and exciting bouquet taking shape.

In photograph (8) below, I've started to add randomly, small sprigs of babies' breath; this is giving me an overall idea of the finished design. At this point, I can see where extra attention and flowers may be needed or added!

8.

As spoken, in photograph (8) above, some gaps have appeared in the babies' breath at the edge of the design. If this happens, select long-stemmed pieces of babies' breath to work into and through the bouquet structure.

Select your sprigs of babies' breath, prior to the placement into your design; keep the stems long; diagram (f) below shows the placements, around and through the bouquet.

f.

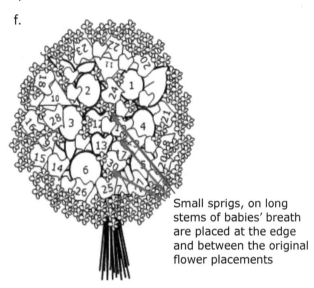

Small sprigs, on long stems of babies' breath are placed at the edge and between the original flower placements

The Handle

Prior to cutting your stems measure your handle length.

g.

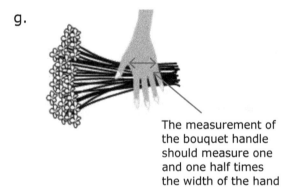

The measurement of the bouquet handle should measure one and one half times the width of the hand

Once you are happy with your design, cut the stems to the appropriate length, finish off as desired.

Hot Tip

When you have completed your bouquet, hold tightly, with the stem ends firmly on the bench, tap the ends onto the bench. This technique evens up your cut stem ends which forms the handle.

Summer Sunshine

A Wired Posy Bouquet Using Australian Native Flowers

This is a fully wired bouquet. Of course, with any of the bouquet designs spoken about in this book, you can modify and adapt many of the techniques.

Flowers and foliage used in this design:

- 3 banksia flowers
- magnolia foliage
- 10 orange mini gerberas
- 3 stems of tiger lilies
- asparagus fern
- sprigs of Australian native foliage

To begin, make sure your flowers and foliage are well conditioned in water prior to wiring.

Wired bouquets can take a bit of time to construct. If made properly, they are secure and the placements can be easier to place when compared with the three previously spoken about bouquets using the flowers and their natural stems.

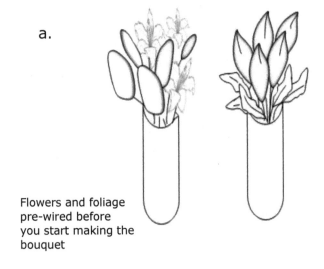

a.

Flowers and foliage pre-wired before you start making the bouquet

The method of wiring for heavy flowers such as banksias: use a 20 gauge x 18 inch (46cm) in the double-leg hairpin

method. Please refer to page 4. Keeping the wire straight, bend in the middle forming two legs, bring the wire across and around the stem of the flower or foliage as shown in the following diagram

The wire and stem end shown before parafilm stem tape is applied.

b.

18 inch (46cm) wire in the double-leg hooked wire method. The wire is bent in two before the hook is bent behind the stem; a single leg of wire is wound three times around both the stem and straight leg of wire.

The wire and stem shown after parafilm stem tape is applied

The two wire legs are then taped with parafilm stem tape to form one leg.

c.

The wired stem and stem end are parafilmed stem taped together to form one; this making for one placement in your design

Seen are the two wire legs without parafilmed stem tape; these wires will form part of the handle for your design

To wire banksias or any other heavy flowers for wired wedding work: leave 1½ inch or (1.27cm) of stem attached to the flower. This length makes for comfortable wiring and for parafilm stem tape to be applied.

Once your flowers and foliage are wired, and ready for use, you can start to construct your design.

The First Three Placements

d.

Each of the three banksia flower stems are individually wired and parafilmed stem taped before they are put into place in the design

By starting with the heavier flowers, you can secure the foundation of your work. The photographs and diagrams below show: two Banksia flowers (photograph 1) are wired ready to be parafilmed stem taped to form one wire leg.

1.

To secure the three Banksia flowers, bind securely with parafilm stem tape: stretch, pull and twist the tape taking it down at least 2/3rds of the wire stem.

Diagram (e) below shows the first three flower placements held between the thumb and the index finger; at this point, you can parafilm stem tape the three placements together if you wish.

e.

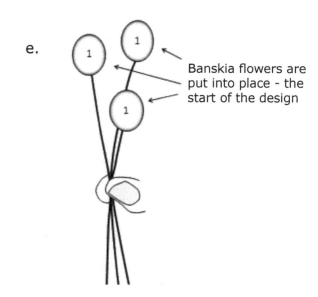

Banskia flowers are put into place - the start of the design

Photograph (2) below shows how a double-leg wired lily flower is put into the centre of the first three originally placed banksia flowers.

2.

Before adding the next placements, make sure your first four placements feel secure in the design. If there is too much movement, it will cause problems as you add more material.

The following diagram shows the lily flower in place

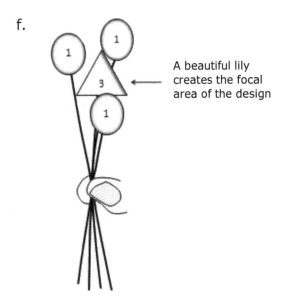

f.

A beautiful lily creates the focal area of the design

The four stems are parafilm stem taped together forming one solid wire stem; this contributes to the second part of the construction of the bouquet handle.

Please remember, these diagrams are two-dimensional, your wedding design is three-dimensional. These diagrams are only guidelines to help you to establish a life-long skill; you will need to practise, practise, practise.

3.

Once you are happy with the first four placements, you can then place your wired and parafilm stem taped foliage into the design.

The foliage needs to be wired in the double-leg, hairpin method. I suggest you use an 18 inch (46cm) x 22 gauge; this will give you nice strong wire which will support your placements.

Please see photograph (3) below. As always, this foliage should be wired and parafilm stem taped prior to constructing the bouquet.

When you are wiring large numbers of leaves or foliage, wire your required number, then parafilm stem tape that number. This method cuts down double-handling and is speed efficient.

Once you are happy with the first four placements, it's now time to place your base foliage into the design.

In photograph (4) below, the base foliage has been added. This foliage gives a nice backdrop to your first placements.

4.

When all of placements feel secure, you are ready to add the next placements.

Please note: bouquets made with such heavy placements can become heavy for your hands and wrists; give yourself rest points, have a tall container handy to rest both your design into and to give your hands and mind a time to rest.

Once you are happy with your work, it's now time to add the extra flowers.

g.

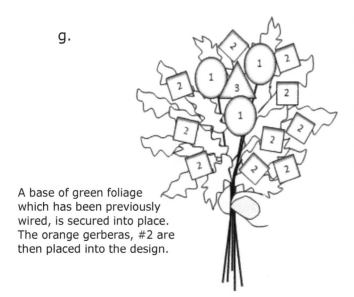

A base of green foliage which has been previously wired, is secured into place. The orange gerberas, #2 are then placed into the design.

Please Note: every fresh flower is different, it's different in size, form and texture, so regardless of how you try, no two bouquets will ever be totally identical.

Working with diagram (g) above and with photograph (5) below, it shows how the actual bouquet starts to emerge. The placements are aesthetically placed throughout the design.

5.

As I bind the placements into place with parafilm stem tape, I leave the tape attached to the roll. Please see the attached tape in photograph (5) below. This method allows me to quickly add my placements.

It's now time to add the lilies. Lily petals are easily broken and by adding the lilies last to your design, you avoid damaging or breaking the petals from the main flower.

h.

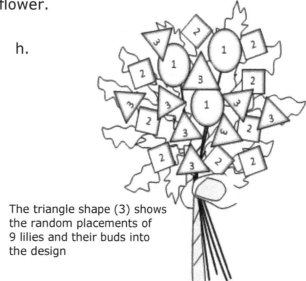

The triangle shape (3) shows the random placements of 9 lilies and their buds into the design

The above diagram will give you some idea of how to hold your design as you work with it.

In photograph (6) below, the profile of the bouquet is seen.

6.

This profile shows a side view of the design while under construction. The parafilm stem tape is attached to the partly made handle of the design.

The tiger lilies are in place in photograph (7) below. All of the placements are added to the work in the same way: one at a time and each placement is measured for its colour, form, size, shape and texture.

7.

Once you are happy with the shape and placement of your flowers, it's time to put the finishing leaves into place.

Having used a softer looking foliage as the base, I'm now using the strength of the magnolia leaf and it's beautiful, brown to red, velvet underside to edge the design. The velvety texture will compliment the masculine texture of the banksia flowers.

Wiring Edging Leaves

8.

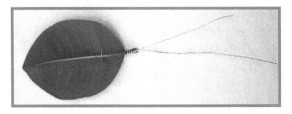

Edging leaves need to be particularly nice as they are the framework of your design.

I wired these leaves with the double-leg hairpin wire. I've used a 22 gauge wire x 18 inches (46cm). Please see Hairpin wiring, page 4.

The wire picks up the main vein of the leaf and is taken about halfway through the vein so that both legs will measure equally when the wires are brought down into the vertical position. Once both wire legs are in the vertical position, one of the wires, as in the hairpin wire on page 4 shows, the single leg is wound two to three times around the short leaf stem and the remaining wire. The wire and stem end are then parafilmed stem taped to form one wire stem.

9

Equally Important

The back of your design is as equally important as the front of your design. To back this design and before I have ribboned the handle into place, I've placed the leaves to back. Please note: some of the leaves have their back to the bouquet giving a nice green finish and some have their beautiful velvety backs showing. Use different ideas in your work – it all helps your design and distinguishes you from other florists or floral artists.

10.

When all of the placements are complete and you have the feeling of satisfaction from within, you will know you have done a good job.

Hot Tip

Clean all leaves with leaf shine or some other cleaner – milk can make a good shining agent and is environmentally safe.

Sunrise And Australian Native Flowers

Chrysanthemum, Calla Lilies and Roses - A Wired And Sectioned Bouquet

If you feel confident enough to work on this bouquet, then why not try to create a bouquet that is similar?

Flowers and foliage used in this design:

- 5 white calla lilies
- 20 pieces of rose-shaped succulent florets
- 10 apricot roses
- 3 white spider chrysanthemums
- 12 heads of Queen Anne's lace
- Cabbage-shaped ivy leaves to back the bouquet

Please Note: With this design, measure each flower length and imagine where its placement will be in your design. Only then, cut, wire and parafilm stem tape the flower or leaf ready for its placement.

The first wiring is with the rose-shaped succulent florets. The florets are heavy in their individual placements so I've used a combination of wiring techniques. Please see the diagrams below:

Single-leg hairpin method and cross wiring:

a.    b.    c.

a. Using the hooked-wire method: the wire is inserted through the thick succulent stem
b. The shorter wire is bent downwards
c. A second wire is inserted cross-ways into and through the stem

d.    e.

d. The second inserted shorter wire is brought down and only one of the longer wire legs is used to wind the three separate legs together.
e. If you are in doubt about the strength of a flower stem and its placement into your bouquet, prior to wiring with your two supporting wires, insert a 20 gauge x 9 inch (23cm) into and up the stem and into the flower head as shown in diagram (e) above.

1.

In photographs (1 - 3), the wiring techniques spoken about in the diagrams can be seen. Succulent stems can be very thick to wire and may need extra wire to support them when put into place.

44

Photograph (2) opposite, four of the twelve succulent stems are wired, then parafilmed stem taped; they are now ready for their placement.

2.

3.

Photograph (3) opposite, shows how the size of the succulent florets are graded; the twelve wired stems are now ready to be parafilmed stem taped to form one stem. Please see diagram (f) below.

In diagram (f), the wired stems of the succulent florets are brought together in your hand. The wire stems are parafilm stem taped to form one wired stem. Once this is done, the stem is ready for placement in your bouquet. Please see photograph (4) opposite page.

f.

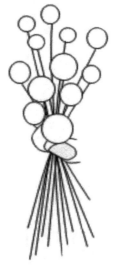

In photograph (4) below, the wire stems are bound with parafilm stem tape. The wired stems now become the bouquet handle, this is been bent downwards and forms the first part of the handle. Please note: when I bend the handle down in these placements, I keep in mind that this placement is a side placement and bend the handle accordingly.

4.

Once the first part of the bouquet construction is complete, place the whole section in a cool area or cold room; do not allow your work to become warm. It's now time to start the second section of your bouquet.

The next section is the wiring and placing of the white calla lily flowers. Each lily has a wire inserted into the stem and up to the flower head. Please re-read diagram (e) on page 44 if you are in doubt about this wiring. The stems are wired in the double-leg hairpin wired method as seen on page (4).

As I work with these more complicated designs, I keep my mind in focus – if your mind wanders from time-to-time, bring it sharply back to the work at hand.

5.

The first smaller lily flower is chosen; this flower has a long, nice curved stem that will add elegance to the bouquet.

The wires are attached and the flower stem is ready to be parafilmed stem taped.

The wires used to insert through the flower stem and into the head of the flower for the double-leg hairpin wire method are both: 20 gauge x 14 inch (35cm).

6.

The five calla lilies are wired and ready to be individually parafilmed stem taped.

Once wired, you may wish to stand your flowers in a container. By doing this, you take the weight pressure off the flower head. Always work on a soft surface when wiring your flowers. I use a soft towel to work on.

In photographs (7 and 8), opposite page, the flowers are seen in their position. Their wire stems have been parafilmed stem taped to form one wired stem and are ready to be bent into position to form part of the handle of the bouquet.

7.

In photograph (8) below, this section of the bouquet is ready to be put into place. The wires are bent downwards, this section is the opposite placement to the succulent placement in photograph (4) on the previous page. I wire my sections, keep them in a cool place, then when all of the sections are ready, I construct my bouquet.

8.

It's now time to wire and parafilm stem tape, your remaining flowers.

9.

In photograph (9), left, Queen Anne's lace has a hollow stem and it can be easy to insert a 22 gauge x 9 inch (23cm) up through the hollow cavity. Once this is done, bend a 9 inch (23cm) wire in two to form a hairpin double-leg wire. Wind the wire as discussed on page 4.

Wiring Chrysanthemums for wedding work is very different to using the flowers in flower arrangements.

Chrysanthemums will easily shatter if they are not handled properly prior to being placed into the wedding design.

A single-leg, hooked wire is used and is seen in diagram (g) below. Carefully penetrate the single-leg of longer wire and push through, but slightly off centre of the chrysanthemum flower, push the longer leg until it comes through the underside of the flower. Continue gently pushing the wire until the curve in the hook sits comfortably over the top and centre of the flower.

In diagram (h) below, marked in red, the bend in the wire sits snugly in the top of the flower.

h.

In diagram (i) below, a double leg, 20 gauge x 9 inch (23cm) wire in the hairpin method has been wound around the flower stem. This technique allows the flower to sit securely once secured into the design.

g.

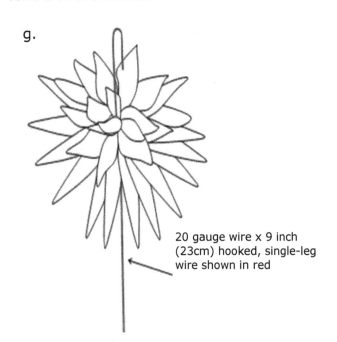

20 gauge wire x 9 inch (23cm) hooked, single-leg wire shown in red

i.

Parafilm stem tape chrysanthemums: start by stretching and applying the tape up close to the flower petals and the underside of the flower calyx. This technique allows the stem and wire to form one wired stem. Stand the wired

47

flower in a container so that the petals don't bruise while you wire and parafilm stem tape your next flowers.

In photograph (10) below, the three white chrysanthemums are seen both wired and parafilm stem taped ready for use within the design

10.

Again: keep all wired flowers in a cool place while other flowers are being prepared.

Note: chrysanthemum stems can be gnarled and woody. If possible, try, clean and smooth the stem before wiring.

Moving now to working with roses. Roses are beautiful flowers in wedding work. To make the most out of the flower, here's another way of wiring and parafilm stem taping them to allow for effective use.

I've measured the stem length that I want to keep attached to the flower before wiring. Then I've inserted 22 gauge x 9 inch (23cm) wire (in red) into the calyx and run the wire parallel with the stem. Please see diagram (j) below.

j.

You will notice the rose leaves have been left attached to the stem; this has been deliberate. The rose leaves, when left on the stem, help to give the rose a natural look once it's secured into the design.

In diagram (k) below, a double-leg, hairpin wire has been attached to the stem of the rose and one of the wire legs has been wound around the rose stem, supporting the wire inserted into the rose calyx. There are now three wire ends shown in the diagram below. This base of wire keeps the flower firm and secure when placed into position.

k.

Diagram (l) below, the rose stem and wires can be parafilm stem taped to form one wire stem.

l.

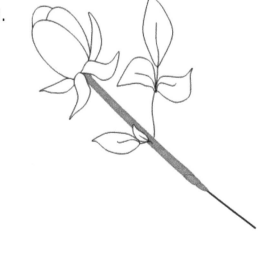

When using parafilm stem tape, remember to *'stretch and pull'* as you twist the stem to secure the tape. As you work towards the attached leaves on the stem, *'stretch, pull'* and work your way around the leaf joints and the stem, still: *'stretching and pulling'*.

In photograph (11) below, one of the single wired roses is ready for its placement within the design. The rose and its leaves give a lovely natural look to the flower.

11.

Joining two sides of your bouquet together

In diagram (m) below, the first section of the bouquet is ready to be joined to the calla lily section as seen in photograph (12), opposite page. In (n), opposite page, the diagram show the first two sections being put together.

m.

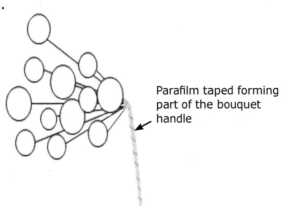

Parafilm taped forming part of the bouquet handle

The wired stems forming the first part of the handle are kept straight and firm. You will need to hold both sections firmly as one is attached to the other.

This bouquet has a back to the design. When placing the two sections together, the back of the placements are kept in mind while both sections are firmly held in your hand.

n.

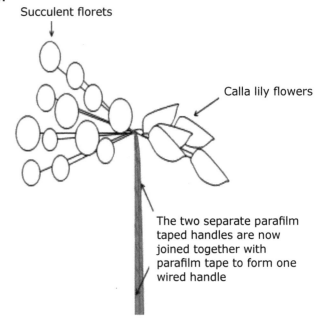

Succulent florets

Calla lily flowers

The two separate parafilm taped handles are now joined together with parafilm tape to form one wired handle

In photograph (12) below, the two sections are joined to form the framework of the bouquet. I have joined these sections with parafilm stem tape. If you feel that this is not secure, use a 26 or 28 gauge wire, holding both sections securely, then bind with the wire before using the parafilm stem tape.

12.

In photographs (4) and (8), I have shown you the two separate sections of the bouquet before they are put together.

With the framework in place, I've added the three white chrysanthemums; these are added as separate placements. By doing this, I can move the flower placement to a suitable position which gives each flower its independent place within the design.

13.

In photograph (13) above, the addition of the white chrysanthemums is clearly seen. The flowers hold their independent place this allows me to work mechanically with the design.

Keep all parafilmed and stem taped placements tidy. Do not allow any pieces of loose tape to be seen, if so, quickly remove.

The junction of the partly made bouquet

14.

In photograph (14) above, the junction of the bouquet is clearly seen. The two side views of the calla lilies and succulent placements are seen held in place with parafilm stem tape and the independent placements of the white chrysanthemums at the junction of the design face upwards giving greater depth to the overall bouquet.

The roses are the next placements. Each rose is added, as the chrysanthemums were, and as separate placements.

In photograph (15), (page 51), the roses are graded in both flower shape and the length of the stem before being cut, wired and parafilm stem taped. Once ready, these flowers are now secured, with parafilm stem tape into their placements within the design.

Below, photograph (15), beautiful apricot roses are added separately to the design.

15.

Below in photograph (16), the parafilm stem taped stems of the roses can be clearly seen.

16.

Following the rose placements, is the placing of the Queen Anne's lace seen in photograph (17) opposite. These are also individually placed to the side of the roses. The flower sections of the bouquet are now readily seen.

In photograph (17) below, the Queen Anne's lace gives an ethereal feeling to the bouquet.

17.

The almost final placement is the placing of the second, wired succulent section seen in photograph (18) below. This section is smaller by comparison to the first section of succulents but is an essential placement to create the visual balance the bouquet needs to add to its creativity.

18.

The large display photograph shows this last placement in place.

Once you are happy with your work, it's
time to ribbon the handle.

The Ribboned Handle

Numbered View
Back of the Design

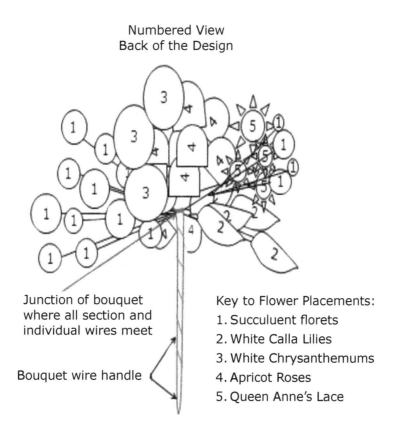

Junction of bouquet
where all section and
individual wires meet

Bouquet wire handle

Key to Flower Placements:

1. Succuluent florets
2. White Calla Lilies
3. White Chrysanthemums
4. Apricot Roses
5. Queen Anne's Lace

Hot Tip

Be very clear in your mind before you
start to construct your design. Such
designs take concentration and
determination.

Apricot Dream

November Lilies and Roses –
A Stunning Bouquet

November lilies and roses in any wedding bouquet make for a beautiful design. The bouquet spoken about in this section is cost-effective to make, and is creative to do. Lilies were the flowers of choice by many artists throughout the centuries. The white lily is often seen in religious paintings when it is used to symbolise the purity of the Virgin's body and the golden anthers reflect the radiance of her soul.

To begin, buy your lilies while the buds have a green tinge; buying the lilies when they are green allows the shape, while conditioning, to open to its natural beauty without damage. The white roses can be bought a few days later.

Flowers and foliage used in this design:

- 6 white November lilies and buds
- 10 white roses
- 1 bunch of red canna lily leaves (each bunch contains about 5 leaves). If canna lily leaves are not available use a suitable leaf which, in its colour, will highlight the white flowers.

Wiring of the first flower is going to be a lily bud. This bud is wired with the same technique as the rose in diagrams: (j, k and l, page 48).

As before, I've measured the stem length that I want to keep attached to the flower before wiring. Then I've inserted a small section of wire: 22 gauge x 9 inch (23cm) wire into the lily base where the calyx sits; the wire runs parallel to the stem. Please see diagram (a), on the opposite page.

a.

Diagram (b) below, the lily stem and wound wire are seen, a doulble-leg hairpin wire is mounted on the base of the stem. The three wires can now be parafilm stem taped to form one wire stem.

b.

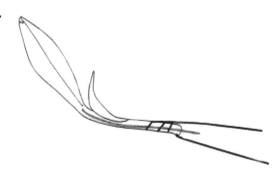

In diagram c, remember, stretch and pull the parafilm stem tape as you twist the stem. Stretch, pull as you work towards the attached leaves on the stem, stretch, pull and work your way around the leaf joints and the stem still stretching and pulling the tape. Stretch your parafilm stem tape to its maximum transparency and twist, attach, twist and attach.

c.

Photograph (1) shows the lily stem with its wire and tape attached.

1

Remember, once wired and taped, keep your flowers fresh by storing them in a cool place.

2.

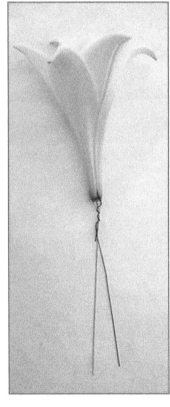

In photograph (2), because of the deep trumpet shape of the lily, the stem has been cut away leaving just a petal joining section at the base of the flower. By doing this, the flower petals remain firm and joined to the remaining stem. Please see the method of cutting and wiring diagrams (d, e and f).

d.

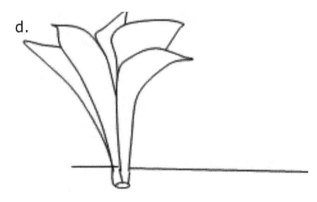

Diagram (d), below left, shows the lily stem almost cut away. A single-leg wire penetrates the flower at its base.

e.

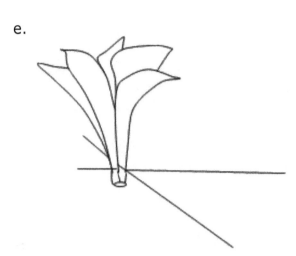

In diagram (e) above, the two single leg wires are seen; these wires will be turned downwards and one of the single, longer legs will secure the three remaining wires into place.

f.

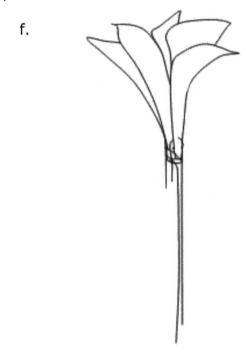

Diagram (f) above, shows how the wiring takes place. Also as a comparison, look at photograph 2 above.

In photograph (3), the first placements are parafilmed stem taped into place. The leaf attached to the lily stem gives a sneaky peek which adds to the character of the design. A cut red canna lily leaf has been secured in its right sequence and then a small, white rose has been added to the design.

3.

previously made sectioned bouquet on page 44, this bouquet consists of one only wired section which forms the trail of the bouquet.

5.

Once the first three to four placements are secured into place, the wired stems are bent downwards to create the first section of the bouquet handle, please observe photograph (5) opposite.

Photograph (4) below: the back side of the bouquet is shown. The canna leaf is wired with the single-leg hooked wire method as described on page 5, diagrams: (a, b, c and d). The photograph gives you an idea of how tightly the parafilm stem tape needs to be pulled to allow for maximum neatness.

Once the handle is in place, it's difficult to rest your work on a flat surface. I use a heavy-based jug with a narrow rim. The jug lip also makes for a secure resting place to hold the bouquet securely. Please see photograph (6), below.

6.

4.

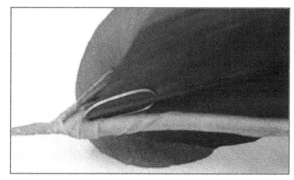

With the first 3 placements in place, the next placement is one of the smaller, wired lilies.

Photograph (5) above, right, shows the trail section of the bouquet. Unlike the

With your work resting securely in the jug, it allows you to pick up and put down with ease. Photograph (7), below shows the next placements of lily flowers.

Junction of the bouquet

 7

In photograph (7), the lilies are placed into the design; each flower has its own place. By cutting the flower stems down to the length described in photograph (2), diagrams: (d, e, and f) of this design, it allows the flowers easy placements within the bouquet.

 8.

Junction of the bouquet

The junction is where all wires meet. Please refer to page 10.

Once the lilies are secured into their placements, you can now add the roses. Again, look at your flowers and keep the best shaped, nicest form for the focal area within the design.

9.

With the roses in place, it's time to add the finishing touches of the Canna leaves. The reds of Canna lilies make for secure backdrops to the different whites of the flowers.

10

11.

Fresh leaves are added to the design.

g.
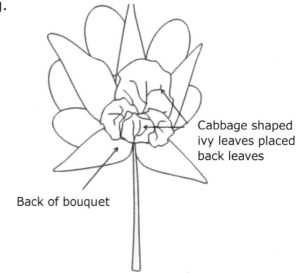

Cabbage shaped ivy leaves placed back leaves

Back of bouquet

Each placement of the flowers and leaves made always meet at the junction of the design. As you place your material into your work, check to see if you are travelling in your placements, if this is so, the placements are not meeting at the junction…!

Not all bouquets have a leaf backing but I have included it in this bouquet.

Leaves can make a nice soft appearance behind the bouquet; in this instance I've used four cabbage shaped ivy leaves to make the backing.

In diagram (g) above, the back of the bouquet is seen. Once the leaves are in place, the ribbon is attached to form the handle. Please see the section: Creating Ribbon Handles For Wedding Designs, pages (11 – 14).

Hot Tip

Many brides prefer simple designs. If you are interviewing a bride, show them this design to begin with and watch their reaction – it may save you time, money and stress!

The Pureness Of White

A Traditional, Wired and Tendril Bouquet

This is advanced floristry work and I would suggest you only try to make this bouquet if you feel you have the confidence to do so!

Such designs are often seen in royal wedding bouquets.

Flowers and foliage used in this design:

- 10 Stems of white and pink hyacinths
- 1 bunch of pink and white lisianthus flowers
- 5 small arum lilies
- 1 bunch of pink spray carnations and their foliage
- 5 cerise cyclamen flowers

Because this is an all-wired bouquet, it's important to wire all of the flowers and foliage before you start to make the bouquet.

In photograph (1) above, I have parafilmed stem taped a small portion of the 24 gauge x 9 inch (23cm) wire which is seen as the top of the hooked area when placed into the centre of the flower. This technique is optional. In many instances, and if the price allows, this method of construction gives a professional finish to your work. You may however, prefer not to parafilm stem tape your wire in the hooked wire construction method. Please see page (7) for this technique of wiring.

1.  2.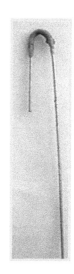

In diagram (2) above, the photograph shows the bent hooked-method of wiring for flower florets. Such hooks can be well prepared in advance. When you have spare moment – parafilm stem tape some 26, 24 x 9 inch (23cm) wires ready for hooking florets...

In photograph (3) below, when the flowers are well conditioned, a number of hyacinth florets can been cut from the main flower stem.

3.

With the wired stems ready for insertion, you can start to wire up the flowers making them ready for use in your design. Once the flowers are wired and parafilm stem taped, place them in a cool place while you wire and prepare your remaining flowers.

In photograph (4) below, the first of many hyacinth florets are wired.

4.

In photograph (5) below, the parafilm stem taped and covered wire in the hooked-wire method is seen. The hook sits tightly in the flowers centre.

5.

6.

Photograph (6) opposite shows three hyacinth florets sitting snugly in one wire stem. This technique of wiring is ideal for traditional wired work where tendrils of flowers are to be used.

In photograph (7) below, a mass of colour is seen in the flowers that are wired, parafilm stem taped and ready to be worked into a tendril shaped wedding bouquet.

7.

Beginning Your Bouquet

I'm using each tendril that I make as a separate placement. Each tendril will contain more than one flower type including different types of foliage. It can be seen in photograph (8) opposite, a tendril is made up with four hooked wired pink hyacinths,

8.

three white hyacinths and a small piece of wired carnation foliage.

The three, separately wired tendrils are parafilmed, stem taped together to form one wired stem; this wired stem is parafilm, stem taped into the design;

each single placement helps to form the backbone of the bouquet.

a.

More tendrils are added, each is parafilmed, stem taped into its place

In diagram (a) above, it shows how to start the bouquet.

b.

For security of the design, I've parafilmed stem taped the joined tenriils to form the 'backbone' before more tendrils are added

In (b) above, more wired and parafilm stem taped tendrils are added. The wires from placements act as supports to the 'backbone' of the wedding bouquet.

In photograph (9) 9. opposite, more tendrils are added.

The adding of tendrils to your first placed wired forms the 'backbone' of your bouquet. This backbone becomes strong and durable with each tendril that is added.

In photograph (9) above, three tendrils have been added; a cyclamen leaf is seen, parafilm stem taped to the 'backbone' of wired material. In the photograph another tendril of pink hyacinths and a cyclamen leaf are about to be parafilm stem taped into the bouquet.

Below, photograph (10), the design starts to take on its own character and your work becomes exciting to create.

10.

Please note: do not get into the habit of twisting your wires when constructing your bouquet – it will detract from the beauty of your work and take from your professional approach to floristry.

In photograph (11) below, the shape and beauty of the bouquet is starting to emerge. More tendrils have been added to the 'backbone' of wiring.

11.

The back of any design is as important as the front. From the back of the design, you can see the importance of keeping your wires straight. In photograph (12) below: it shows how the tendrils come together to form very neat placements and construction in the design of this bouquet.

The Back View Of A Wired Tendril Bouquet

12.

As the design grows in proportion and design, you will need to make a decision of where the junction of your bouquet will be? When this is done, you need to sharply bend downwards, the whole of the wire construction you have been working on. In photograph (13), below, the junction of the design is clearly seen.

13.

Once you have decided on the place of the junction and the wires are bent into a downwards position, this forming the bouquet handle, you can start to create the top section of the bouquet.

I continually use a heavy jug with a wide opening to rest my bouquet in. by doing this, I give my hands a rest and it allows me to see the whole design as I'm constructing it.

In photograph (14) below, the junction is clearly seen while the bouquet handle sits in the jug.

14.

In photograph (15) below, the first of the top tendrils have been added to the design also, extra tendrils are added at the top section of the bouquet.

15.

In photograph (16) below, the design is almost completed. I'm now adding some base flowers of miniature pink carnations. These flowers have been wired and parafilm stem taped into position. These flowers will add to the extra depth of colour that is required to make this bouquet the striking design it will become.

16.

In photograph (16) above, the mini carnation placements are in place, now, I'm ready to 'top up' the bouquet. Secure your bouquet in your supporting container, as explained previously, I have used a glass jug in this instance. Once

secure, prepare some tendrils that will suite your bouquet design to 'top up'. These tendrils can be a little bunchy, you may also include some of your feature flowers. Some of my feature flowers are: pink and white lisianthus, cyclamen, calla liles with small insertions of pink and white hyacinths.

The Profile Of The Bouquet

17.

The profile of the bouquet above shows how many tendrils, and in some instances, some separate flowers have been added. The bouquet is full and interesting to look at.

The Back, Top Section Of The Made Bouquet

In photograph (18) next page, the back of the bouquet before ivy leaves are wired and parafilm, stem taped into place; these form a backing to the design.

18.

Hot Tip

By making use of the flowers in season, beautiful bouquets can be made with affordable flowers.

Please note

All wires added to the junction of the design are kept as straight as possible. Parafilm stem taped wires are secured into the main handle of the design.

The advantage of using this method of construction in bouquet design allows a bouquet to be made to any size (large or small), a great number of different flowers can be used including:

- lily of the valley
- gardenias
- roses (miniatures and some larger varieties)
- freesia
- tulips (smaller rather that the large varieties)
- hyacinths
- daffodils and bluebells
- Singapore orchids
- Especially lovely is a bouquet made of white and cream flowers.

A Royal Wedding Bouquet

Proteas and The Self-Stem Bouquet

Many brides like the combination of protea flowers and natural foliage in their bouquet. Such flowers make a nice autumn or winter design and compliment velvet fabrics or other similar heavy textured materials.

With texture, none of the textures used in this design are feminine; that is part of the appeal.

Flowers and foliage used in this design:

- 3 largish deep pink proteas
- 15 red leucadendrons
- A variety of mixed native foliage

To begin any self-stem bouquet, I lay my lower section of foliage out on a flat surface. By doing this, I can identify the length required. Please study photograph (1) below.

1.

I then lay the top section of foliage down, photograph (2), to estimate the overall length of the design.

2.

I cut my foliage to the required length. On a double-leg, hairpin wire, I wire all of the foliage making it ready to parafilm stem tape those wired stems. The wire gauge used for such heavy material is 20 gauge x 18 inches (46cm).

In photograph (3) below, the cut, wired and parafilm stem taped wires are seen at the base joined as one. This base forms the junction of the bouquet.

Junction of design

3.
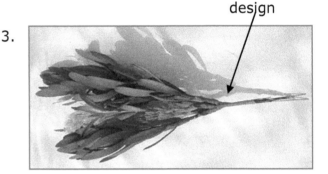

In photograph (4) below, it shows the wired top section; these stems, once I'm happy with the size of the overall design, will be parafilmed stem taped ready for placement into the design.

4.

Remember, the overall length of the foliage must represent the size of the flowers being used. Proteas can be large and physically heavy to work with.

The protea bouquet

a.

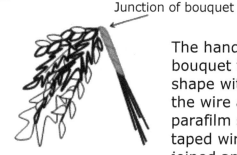

Junction of bouquet

The handle of the bouquet takes shape with all of the wire and parafilm stem taped wires joined and becoming as one

b.

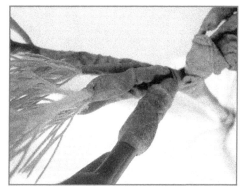

Junction of bouquet where both sections meet

Both the top and lower sections of the bouquet are brought together to form one design

The wire section, where the junction's bend exists, has been turned downwards; this section is now the start of the bouquet handle.

In photograph (5) below, the top section is wired into place with the bottom section creating one bouquet. Both sections are held tightly with parafilm stem tape; this secures the top section of the design. Both sections are parafilm stem taped to form the handle, please see diagram (b) on the opposite page.

5.

In photograph (6) below, the joining of the two sections is clearly seen.

6.

Once the top and lower sections are in place, you can start to add the side placements. These are measured, cut, wired and then parafilm stem taped before they are placed into your design.

In photograph (7) on the next page, the outline of the bouquet is clearly seen. It is now critical, before placing your flowers or foliage into the focal area: *measure each stem, cut, wire and parafilm stem tape each flower for its own specific placement.*

With larger flowers like proteas, you may need to use two double-leg hairpin wires of the same gauge: 20 gauge x 18 inches (46cm) to keep them secure in your design.

The overall shape of the bouquet is seen prior to the focal placements.

7.

In diagram (c) on the opposite page, the skeleton and outline of the bouquet is seen. The proteas are added by following the numbers. Please take note: each flower is individually measured, the stem is cut, then wired and parafilm stem taped; once this is done, each wired stem is singly taped into the junction of the bouquet. Keep your wires straight; do not twist as you join all of the wired stems to form the handle.

Skeleton Of The Bouquet

c.

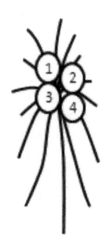

Proteas 1, 2, 3 and 4 are securely wired and parafilm stem taped into place

When you are happy and these placements and they feel secure in your hand, you can add the lighter foliage or flowers you are using.

Please use one of the methods mentioned in this book to finish off the back of the bouquet. Your bouquet is now ready for use.

Hot Tip

When buying or picking proteas, banksias or any heavy headed flowers, chose the smaller heads and look for the thinner stems. Some proteas have exceedingly large stems; this will make it very difficult to work the flowers into the design.

Protea Profusion

The Wired and Self-Stem Bouquet

There's a trend towards loose, woody and leafy bouquets in 2018. This bouquet takes a lot of thinking about but once your mind is clear and you understand how you are going to make the design, it can come together very quickly.

Flowers and foliage used in this design:

- silver birch foliage in small, wispy branches
- 4 white phalaenopsis orchids left attached to their growing stem
- sprigs of white star jasmine
- 10 small white iceberg roses
- 3 small gardenias
- 3 pieces of pine lace.

You will need to prepare, clean and wire your flowers ready for the construction into the bouquet.

I.   With the flowers and foliage you have, now create the design in your mind, before you start to construct your actual wedding bouquet.

II. In diagram (a) opposite, make sure all of your flowers and foliage are wired before creating the trail of your bouquet.

III. If the foliage needs to be cleaned or roses need to have their weather petals removed, this is done before wiring your flowers and before you start to make your bouquet. (Please see page 25, re weather petals).

Wired flowers and leaves ready to be added to the bouquet as it's constructed.

a.

To begin, the lose trail of the bouquet is first put into place. Please follow the following photographs and diagrams:

1.

Soft birch foliage is available in spring time but you can substitute with trailing ivy stems, some tropical trailing vine plants and other freely growing trailing plants.

Once you are happy with the pieces of foliage for the trail of the bouquet, bind securely all of the ends of the trails with 20 gauge wire Please see diagram (b), on the opposite page.

71

In photograph (2) below, some of the leaves have been taken off the stems to show the naked branches. By doing this, it shows an artistic flair to the work. Some extra loops of birch are added to the hanging leaf fronds.

b. Bind the meeting wires securely

c. Bring the stem ends securely into the handle

d. Extra curved stems of birch are added giving a wispy look to the design, once this is done, parafilm, stem tape to create the first part of the bouquet handle.

b. Bind securely with 20 gauge florist wire

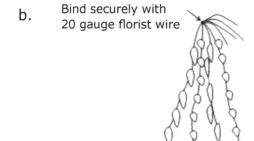

c. Bind the newly made handle securely with 20 gauge wire

d. Once the stems are secure, bind with parafilm stem tape

Extra curved stems of birch are added to the design, this now starts to create the overall shape of the wedding bouquet.

When you are establishing the overall shape of the bouquet the next critical step in creating your design is the top or upper section of the bouquet.

The Focal Area or Point Of Interest And The Upper Area Of Your Design

e.

Wires meet at the focal area of the bouquet

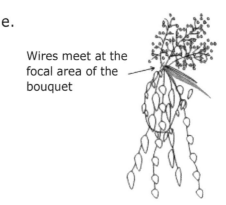

In the above diagram (e) on page 72, the red cross indicates the focal area where all of the wired flowers and foliage stems meet. The diagram shows three pieces of pine lace securely in place. The pine was previously wired, along with the other flowers and foliage before the construction of the bouquet took place.

The pine is wired with the single-leg hooked method on a 22 gauge x 9 inch (23cm) wire

You are now ready to move on. The next placement in this bouquet is the stem of phalaenopsis orchids. With this orchid placement, I'm keeping the orchids on their original growing stem. Measure the stem and ask yourself, *'is this stem of orchids' right for this bouquet and this placement?'*

If you feel satisfied with your own response, the placement will sit nicely in the design.

Creating The Focal Area Of Your Bouquet

f.

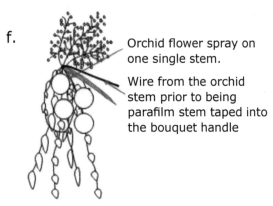

Orchid flower spray on one single stem.

Wire from the orchid stem prior to being parafilm stem taped into the bouquet handle

In diagram (f) above, all of the wired stems radiate from the junction of the bouquet.

The placement of the orchid stem is the first to draw the attention of the eye towards the focal area.

g.

Three small gardenia flowers are ready to be placed into the design.

The wired stems are still exposed and not parafilmed stem taped into position

The three small gardenia flowers have been wired in the double-leg method as spoken of on page (4).

h.

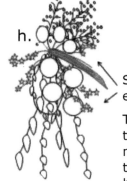

Star Jasmine leading the eye to the focal area

The red wires indicating the jasmine wire still needs to be parafilm taped into the design handle

Tendrils of star jasmine are placed at four separate sections leading the eye more predominately towards the focal area you are creating. The method of wiring for the jasmine is the single-leg hooked method.

All wires used in this bouquet must be parafilmed stem taped before being placed in your wedding design.

i.

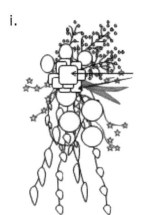

A group of 10 roses is made into a posy shape and then inserted into the focal area of the bouquet

The posy shape wires are wired as one wired stem, this is seen in this diagram

The square cube shapes represent the roses in the bouquet. Please follow the diagrams below to construct the posy shape needed to insert into the focal area of your design.

j.

Nine of the roses, which have previously been wired, parafilmed stem taped, are grouped as one as seen in this diagram

In the above (j) the parafilmed, stem taped wires are kept straight.

k.

The fuller rose is placed into the centre of the nine roses and the ten stems are parafilmed stem taped together to form one stem

The secured posy of ten roses is now ready to be placed into the focal area of the wedding bouquet. This simple technique can save a lot of time and stress and saves many difficult placements being made within the design.

l.

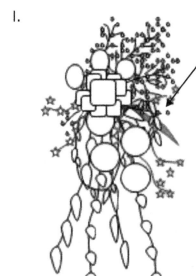

Extra pieces of foliage and birch loops can be added to finish off the bouquet. The birch loops would need to be wired in the single-leg hooked wire method at this point.

The completed wire handle can now be ribboned up and the bouquet finished off.

To finish off the handle of the bouquet: wind tightly with a matching ribbon to the flowers or the bride's gown.

Hot Tip

Spring and new foliage can droop very quickly once it's cut and put into a wedding design. Look for the deepest green in the foliage of your choice; do not pick new shoots for any wedding work.

Ready For The Bride

In the wedding bouquet section I ha ve spoken about many different approaches to making wedding bouquets; if you think your design through before making your bouquet, you can mix and match many of the techniques discussed in this book. Having said that, be careful not to make your work cumbersome and heavy by using different techniques which don't suit your material or the design.

Semi-Crown of Babies Breath

Making a semi-crown shape can be done by creating your own wire shape. The shape is created by binding 3 x 18 gauge x 18 inch (46 cm) wires together with parafilm stem tape to form one frame. Once you have the wires as one length, then measure the size of the head of the wearer. If you prefer, you can by headdress shapes on line.

Flowers used in used in this design:

- 1 bunch of well conditioned babies' breath
- 1 roll of fine fuse, florist binding or hobby wire

In diagram (a) below, I have made the headdress shape shown.

a.

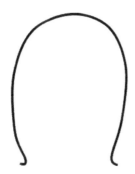

However, I have also bought the shape in photograph (1) below on line.

To wire the babies' breath onto the frame and to stop it unravelling, please follow the next steps:

- Lay the wire about 2 inches (5 cm) along the side of the frame, please follow the red wire in diagram (b) below:

b.

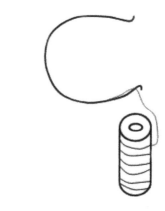

- In (c), take the wire and curve it for form a 'V' shape so that the wire comes back on itself.

c.

- Twist the wire around the shape you have chosen to work with making sure it's secure and will not unfasten

You are now ready to start adding the babies' breath. The human head is one of the hottest parts of the human body therefore your flowers should be well conditioned for at least 24 hours in deep water before you start to use the fresh flower or leaf material in any construction work.

Cut small bunches of babies' breath and use as follows:

- In diagram (d) a small bunch of babies' breath is held between the finger and thumb. The wire is shown in red.

d.

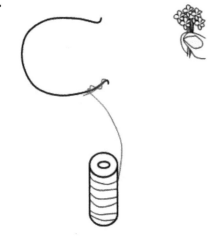

- In diagram (e), the first small bunch of babies' breath is wired to the frame.

e.

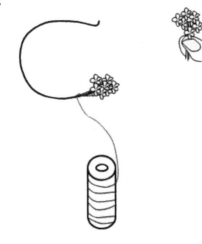

More small bunches, of a similar size and shape of flowers are again selected, cut and made ready to add to your design.

- Diagram (f) shows more small bunches of babies' breath added to the frame

f.

Photograph (2) below shows the actual design under construction.

2.

Keep the end stems of your babies' breath short as you construct the design. By doing this, you will eliminate a chunky appearance at the back of your work – create your work in small bunches as spoken about in diagrams: (d, e and f).

In photograph (3) below, the head crown is almost complete.

3.

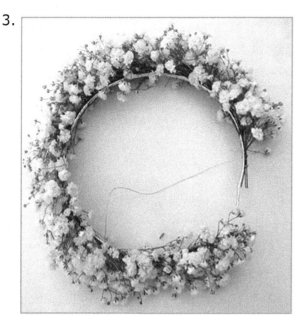

To complete your design you will need to work with a glue gun.

g.

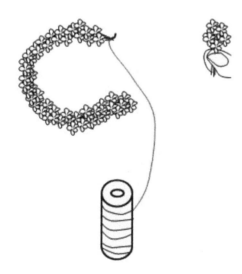

To finish off the design, twist the wire and bring it back on itself as you did at the start – the same principle of wiring will keep you design tight and safe

Choose small bunches of babies' breath, surround with a small dab of glue from the hot glue gun and place onto your

design where your wire has been tied. Please see diagram (h) below. Work your babies' breath from the outside to the inside.

h.

By working with the hot glue gun and the babies' breath from the outside to the inside, you end up with a neat and well finished piece of work. Please see diagram (i) below.

i.

In diagram (j) below, the completed semi-crown; the slightly fuller side profile gives an elegant slant to this simple design.

Hot Tip
Try to buy smaller flowered babies' breath, this makes for a softer look in the finished design.

A Touch of Elegance For A Garden Wedding

Making a Simple Floral Crown

To begin the floral crown, you will need:

- 4 by 18 gauge or 6 x 20 gauge wires.
- If available use 18 inch (46 cm) lengths. Please note, if not available; use what is on hand and cut to the required length
- Florist parafilm stem tape, and
- 1 roll of fine fuse, florist binding or hobby wire.

To make sure the crown fits the head of the wearer, you may choose to measure the shape once it is made.

The full measurement for this crown is 50cm or 20 inches in circumference.

To make the shape:

Choose half the number of wires you have available. If you are using 18 gauge use 2; if you are using 20 gauge use 3. If you have 20 gauge x 46cm that would be perfect, however, you may need to adapt shorter wires and adjust them to the required length.

a) Put your wires together: side by side to tape and make one single leg – if you are using shorter wires, do not tape to the end of the wire; you will need some exposed wire to attach the next wires.

Please note: if I have to join shorter wires, I slightly stagger the wires giving a stepping appearance; this technique allows a smoother appearance when parafilm stem tape is applied.

b) Holding firmly, run the tape – stretching and pulling, as you secure the wires to make one wire leg.

c) **If using shorter wires**: the first section of the frame is created by securing them with parafilm stem tape.

When you are close to the end of securing the first wires, add the next wires; this will form a longer length. The second wires sit side by side forming the required length.
Once you have the four wires joined together it will make one wire length.

Joining the wires

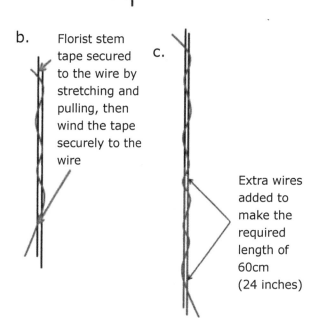

a. Florist stem tape secured to the wire by stretching and pulling, then wind the tape securely to the wire

b. Florist stem tape secured to the wire by stretching and pulling, then wind the tape securely to the wire

c. Extra wires added to make the required length of 60cm (24 inches)

Once the wires are parafilm stem taped together, you are ready to make the crown shape.

d) The shape of the frame is made by gently manipulating the wire into position. When you are happy with the size and shape you have created, join the ends by: stretch and pulling the parafilm stem tape while holding the two ends tightly with your fingers and thumbs. Massage the stretched tape as you attach it to make sure the joining ends are secure.

d.

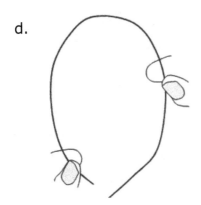

e) The crown shape is ready for the flowers to be added.

e.

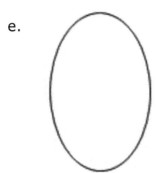

Flowers used in used in this design:

- 20 small pink roses
- small rose or ivy leaves if available.

To begin, make sure your flowers and foliage are well conditioned, then, wire the roses and some leaves individually; these are used as separate placements.

If the rose calyx is large, you may need to cut a small section away, by doing this you will allow the rose to sit within the design. In diagram (f) below, the section is shown.

Cutting away part of the calyx

f.

Rose calyx ⟶

Cutting line ⟶

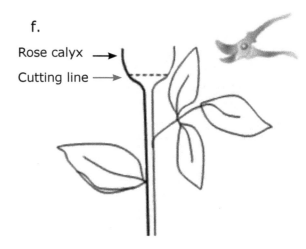

Keeping the centre point of the frame you are working on in mind, attach your flowers by using the binding wire you are going to use. The first flowers are wired to the frame. When each placement is secured, cut off the remaining excess wire.

Excess wire is cut away

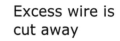

1.

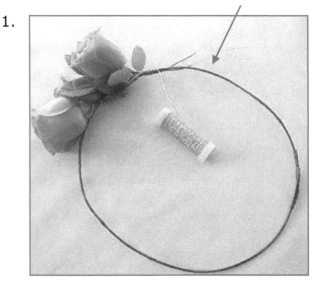

By cutting the excess wire off as you add your placements of flowers, it keeps your frame nice and clean and allows you to work the remaining ends into the design.

Continue to add the roses alternating the different shapes. If your roses are mixed in sizes, you need to avoid having all one size in one place!

In photograph (2) below, the partly made design is clearly seen.

When you have reached the centre of the frame, stop, wind the wire once or twice around the last placement of rose or leaves and the frame, then cut your binding wire leaving a reasonable length. Having this wire left attached will reduce stress when you want to complete your design, by using this technique, the wire is there if you should need it...!

In diagram (g) above and opposite, the partly made crown is seen with the binding wire attached to the reel. Some floral artists cut off a length of wire and work with that; I sometimes leave the wire attached to the reel to give me flexibility with the wiring.

The partially made crown of flowers

g.

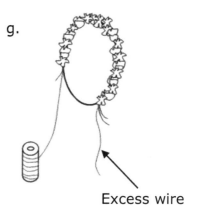

Excess wire

Cut excess wires from your design when you are happy the placements are secure.

To complete your design: when there are sufficient flowers and leaves secured to the design, it's time to finish. I wind the wire in and around the frame and back through the flowers and leaves. This anchors the wires into the design. If you wish, you can put a small dob of hot glue on the ends of the wire and push them securely into the back of your wiring.

In diagram (h) below, shows finishing off the design by winding the wire in and through the last placements. The lower and part section of the design is seen with the wires, outlined in red.

h.   Diagram finishing off the
                          design

If you are unsure about the size of the head of the wearer of the crown, you can always make a shape as described above but leave the wires open with a hook that can be made to fit either for a larger or smaller size.

i.

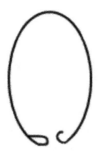

Please follow the instruction above from (a) to (e).

Pretty In Pink

Rose Corsage

Corsages are still popular and remarkably, young people still like to wear the corsage for graduations and other functions.

Among the most popular flowers, roses still hold their own as the flower chosen of choice.

Flowers used in this design:

- 4 red roses
- 6 rose leaves

To begin, choose 4 nice smallish red roses. There is one of two ways to wire your roses to make a corsage.

1. Choose which method of wiring you are going to use: is it
    a. single-leg – vertical wired method or
    b. single-leg hairpin wire?

In photograph (1) below, I have chosen method (b) to wire the roses.

1.

In method (b), the shorter leg of wire penetrates the calyx; the wire is taken through to the opposite side, brought down and the longer wire is used to wind

around both the short rose stem and shorter wire. For more information, please see page (6) single leg wiring for calyx wiring.

Once wired, in photograph (2) below, the roses are parafilmed stem taped and made ready for use.

2.

In photograph (3) below, I wire the leaves ready for the corsage construction. The photograph shows the backside of the leaf.

3.

The leaves are then taped with parafilm stem tape.

Please Note: Wiring of ribbons and any sundry items such as loops of pearls and ribbon loops for any bouquet construction can be done well in advance

The bows below were made using the following techniques:

Making the Two-Sided Bow

You will need about 12 inches (30cm) ribbon to make the two-looped bow below:

a.

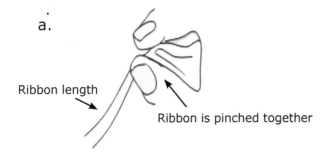

Ribbon length

Ribbon is pinched together

Following the directions in (b), create a second loop. Keep your loops small, remember, you are making a corsage.

b. The second loop for the bow is created

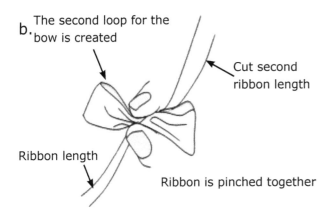

Cut second ribbon length

Ribbon length

Ribbon is pinched together

Cut the ribbon so that there are two small lengths as seen in the photograph.

Wire the loop with the single-leg method as shown in diagram (c) opposite page.

Follow the instructions in diagram (c) (d) to secure the ribbon with florist wire.

c.

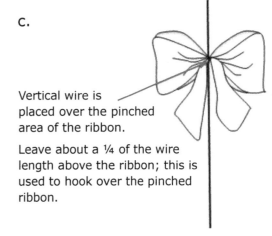

Vertical wire is placed over the pinched area of the ribbon.

Leave about a ¼ of the wire length above the ribbon; this is used to hook over the pinched ribbon.

d.

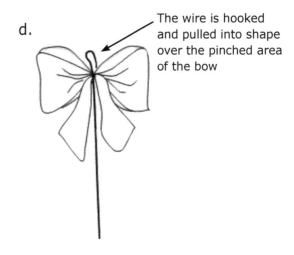

The wire is hooked and pulled into shape over the pinched area of the bow

e.

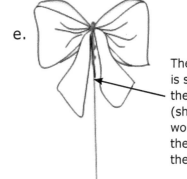

The short leg of wire is shown in black; the longer leg of wire (shown in red) is wound twice around the short leg securing the bow in place.

The smaller bow consists of two loops and two end as shown in diagram (f) below.

f.

The ribbon is pinched together before securing the single-leg hooked wire method in diagram (g).

g.

The above directions are relatively easy to do it's the actual construction of the corsage that takes learning and developing the skill that takes time to perfect.

The wired bows as described in diagrams (a. – g.).

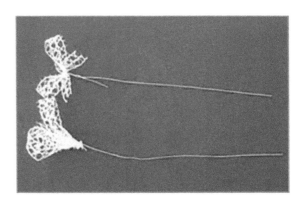

Once the ribbons are wired, keeping the wires separate, the wires are parafilmed stem taped and made ready to use.

Making the corsage

Starting with the first three placements, make sure that all three wires join at the focal point shown in diagram (h) below.

h.

The first three placements are in place joining at the focal area. The placements consist of: two wired leaves and the second made bow

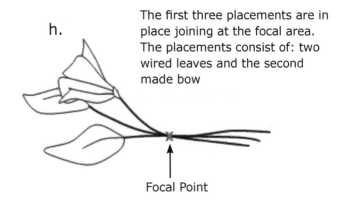

Focal Point

Continue to add the roses, leaves and ribbon as shown in diagram (i) shown on the next page.

The placements of the material

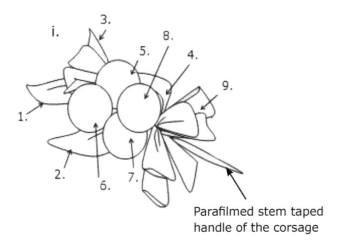

Parafilmed stem taped handle of the corsage

Now please follow the numbers:

Please Note: keep all of the wire meeting at the focal point between your thumb and finger as you construct the corsage.

1. The first leaf is put into place
2. The second leaf is placed a little lower than the first leaf – each leaf meets at the focal point, see (h.)
3. The first bow is put into place, please see (h) page 87.
4. A third leaf is put into place a little lower but still joins at the focal point.

Remember: keep all of the wires between your finger and thumb as you construct the corsage.

5 The first rose placement is placed into the corsage, still with the wires meeting at the focal point, please refer back to diagram (i.)
6 The second rose is put into place, again, the wires meeting at the focal point
7 The third rose is put into place, meeting the wire at the focal point

8 The fourth rose is added to the design. When looking at your focal point flowers, keep the nicest and best flowers for this placement
9 The Two-Sided bow is put into place; this wire also meets at the focal point.

When you are happy with your placements, secure all of the wired and parafilmed stem taped stems by binding with parafilm stem tape to form the corsage handle. Now add a pearl or diamante head pin to secure to clothing

Corsage – Back View

Diagram (j) shows the corsage being held between the thumb and index finger and is where all of the wired flowers and foliage meet.

Back View Of The Made Corsage

j.

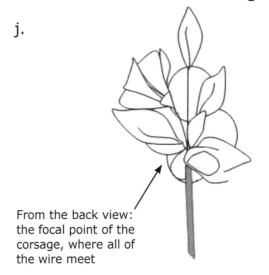

From the back view: the focal point of the corsage, where all of the wire meet

Hot Tip

To begin, choose sturdy and robust flowers to make your first corsages. You can move to making corsages with delicate flowers once you gain the skills, technique and confidence to move to advanced work.

The Rose Corsage

Rose Buttonhole

If a buttonhole is required for a male to wear, a rose buttonhole is one of the best choices. You can add other material such as Heather or fine fern if you wish. In this demonstration, I'm using just one rose bud and three rose leaves.

Flowers used in this design:

- 1 red rose bud
- 3 rose leaves

Before you start to make your design, make sure the rose leaves are clean and unmarked.

In diagram (a) below, wire your three leaves in the single-leg, hooked method.

a.

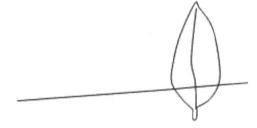

In diagram (b), bring the shorter leg of wire down into a vertical placement, then bring the longer leg of wire down and wind twice around the short rose leaf stem and the shorter section of wire. Now wire the two remaining rose leaves in the same method.

b.

Diagram (c) below, shows how the wiring of the rose leaf should look prior to parafilm stem tape being applied.

c.

Leave about 1 inch (2.5cm) of stem attached to the rose and cut the remaining stem away.

The rose is wired in the single-leg, hairpin wire technique. By wiring in this way, it secures the rose head if it should be knocked. Please see page (6), single-leg hairpin wire through the calyx wiring method.

When your four placements are wired, parafilm stem tape them ready for creating your design.

In photograph (1) below, your placements are now ready to be worked into the design.

1.

90

Diagram (d) below, it shows the four wired stems held between the index finger and thumb, by doing this, your placements are secure. Once you are happy with your work, you can parafilm, stem tape them together to form one wired stem. When this is done, cut the wired stems to no longer 1½ inches (1.27cm). If the wire ends feel a little rough, re-parafilm stem tape the stem again.

d.

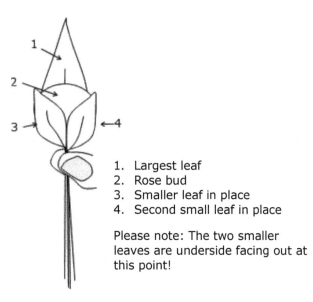

1. Largest leaf
2. Rose bud
3. Smaller leaf in place
4. Second small leaf in place

Please note: The two smaller leaves are underside facing out at this point!

Now you are at this point, parafilm stem taple your wires to form one stem which becomes your handle for the buttonhole. You are now ready to turn down the two smaller rose leaves.

Diagram (e) shows the two smaller leaves now turned down.

e.

In photograph (2) below, you can see the two smaller wired leaves are in the downturned position. To finish off the buttonhole, insert a pearl headed pin into the wired stem of the design.

2.

Hot Tip
Corsages and buttonholes can be made a day in advance: once made lightly spray with fresh water. Spray some tissue paper with water; lay the corsage on the tissue, cover with more lightly sprayed tissue and store in a cool place.

Acknowledgements:

Femal Face Image:
<a href="http://clipartmag.com/female-face-outline">Female Face Outline</a>

FULL POTENTIAL TRAINING

*Full Potential Training is the Working Partner to
Books For Reading On Line.Com*

Full International Accreditation (CPD)

ACCREDITED COURSE – FAST TRACK COMMERCIAL FLORISTRY

A 20 WEEK TRADE COURSE

AVAILABLE IN AUSTRALIA AT DESIGNATED DATES

If you loved our last book: **How To Create Easy Flower Arranging**, you will love How **To Create Easy Wedding Bouquets**.

The book contains step-by-step instruction in HOW TO make a range of different Bouquets. It contains over 108 colourful photographs, and over 180 figurative drawings for you to follow.

It is easy to learn the *industry secrets* with this **NEW** approach to an age-old art form.

Published by Books For Reading On Line.Com

(www.booksforreadingonline.com)

Australia

Distributed by Books For Reading On Line.Com
(www.booksforreadingonline.com)
Australia

CPSIA information can be obtained
at www.ICGtesting.com
Printed in the USA
BVHW022014190421
605310BV00014B/945